sharing the
blue
crayon

How to Integrate Social, Emotional, and Literacy Learning

MARY ANNE BUCKLEY

Stenhouse
PUBLISHERS

Portland, Maine

Stenhouse Publishers
www.stenhouse.com

Credits
Figure 8.1: © 2012 Larry Lamsa, https://www.flickr.com/people/larry1732/

Library of Congress Cataloging-in-Publication Data
Buckley, Mary Anne.
  Sharing the blue crayon : how to integrate social, emotional, and literacy learning / Mary Anne Buckley.
  pages cm
Includes bibliographical references and index.
  ISBN 978-1-62531-011-8 (pbk. :alk. paper) -- ISBN 978-1-62531-041-5 (ebook) 1. Emotions.
2. Social learning. 3. Learning--Social aspects. 4. Group work in education. 5. Literacy--Study and teaching. I. Title.
  LB1073.B83 2014
  370.15'23--dc23

                                                                    2014030651

Cover design, interior design, and typesetting by Alessandra S. Turati
PRINTED ON 30% PCW
RECYCLED PAPER
Manufactured in the United States of America

21 20 19 18 17 16 15   9 8 7 6 5 4 3 2 1

To my son, Griffin, whose tender honesty
and ability to see the Light in everyone
guides my every step

CONTENTS

ACKNOWLEDGMENTS

My entire teaching career has been a collaborative endeavor. Every student, every teacher, every administrator has taught me something. I am so grateful to Bailey's Elementary for . . . being Bailey's. I cannot put into words the power of the Bailey's community, but for all of you who are part of it, please accept my deepest thanks for sharing your time, talent, and treasures with me.

I give extra thanks to these exceptional people who guided my way.

Emelie Parker and Tess Pardini—for the walks, talks, and wisdom. You are the cornerstones of my teaching philosophy.

Kathy Twombly—who knew so many Truths could be found in a cup of cappuccino?

Lauren Nye Schrum, LRN—for the questions (especially the one that started this book).

Melissa Fleischer—for letting Kent's little sister come to your trailer to observe your class for two hours and for the twelve years of learning and laughing that followed. Your classroom continues to be my standard for creating peaceful and powerful communities.

Christy Hermann Thompson—for your endless desire to make the curriculum relevant and engaging for our students. It is an honor to teach, learn, and grow with you.

Kent Buckley-Ess—for suggesting I come to Bailey's in the first place. Once again, you displayed your exceptional gift of subtly guiding teachers to finding their own greatness. Thank you (and Julie) for everything.

Holly Holland—you watched Writing Workshop for an hour and saw the passion in my heart for teaching. You clarified my intention, focused my purpose, took my wild rambles and found the nuggets worth keeping. Thank you—and everyone at Stenhouse—for keeping children the focus of our profession.

Shawn—for the kumquat.

Introduction

For eleven years, I taught at Bailey's Elementary School in Northern Virginia. During the time I was there, teaching kindergarten through second grade, the school's one thousand three hundred students came from forty different countries and spoke thirty different languages at home. The test scores of our kindergarten students on average fell 3.5 deviation points below the state average. As teachers and administrators, we worked diligently to close those academic gaps. But we also found that in addition to their weak preparation for academic work, students from second-language homes struggled to initiate and participate in conversations, take turns with other children, make connections between school topics and life experiences, and seek and give clarification. In short, they lacked the tools of social, emotional, and academic language.

In response, I developed a program for my classroom that I call Friendship Workshop. I created it because I saw more and more of my students stalled in their learning due to their inexperience handling respectful interactions with peers and adults. Their disputes at the science table and arguments on the playground, their tears after buddy reading, and their hurtful jeers when someone acted differently all stemmed from not understanding their emotions or how to express their needs accurately. I continued to refine Friendship Workshop over the years because I saw how it supported me in developing the readiness skills that children from all backgrounds need to contribute to their own learning. In a sense, it gives students the language to learn.

We practice specific interpersonal (social) and intrapersonal (emotional) interactions during Friendship Workshop, and these lessons are the foundation of everything we do as readers and writers. We learn how to tell a story and how to listen and respond to another's tale. We discover the power of emotions and word choices, not just in literature but also in our lives. We share, which builds empathy and trust and leads to problem solving and revision. The social-emotional skill development does not represent a one-time lesson or a tagalong activity. Rather, the integrated approach to learning how to learn runs fluidly throughout the school day, reinforcing each child's individuality while also helping all students relate to the curriculum in genuine ways.

Lev Vygotsky, Jean Piaget, and John Dewey all established that the most successful learning is social in nature. According to Vygotsky, "Every function in the child's cultural development appears twice: first, on the social level, and later, on the individual level; first, between people (interpsychological) and then inside the child (intrapsychological)" (1978, 57). Dewey added, "I believe that we violate the child's nature and render difficult the best ethical results, by introducing the child too abruptly to a number of special studies, of reading, writing, geography, etc., out of relation to this social life. I believe, therefore, that the true centre of correlation of the school subjects is not science, nor literature, nor history, nor geography, but the child's own social activities" (1897, 10).

As a primary grades teacher, I believe it is my job to initiate all children into the community of school. At first I thought that oral language practice and item knowledge such as vocabulary, grammar, and syntax were all that young students needed in order to communicate and become part of a literate classroom community. I soon learned that the social and emotional languages we use when connecting and communicating were equally important.

To teach and reinforce the building blocks of literacy, we must show our students how to interact with others, develop self-control and persistence, and find their own voices as well as value the contributions of peers. These social-emotional skills must be explicitly shared and practiced. They can't be viewed as add-ons to the curriculum or as occasional lessons we use as icebreakers during the first days of school. For many of our students, these crucial life lessons may be the only way into the academic life.

Although a large portion of our teaching in the primary grades involves checking off numerous curriculum requirements, we know that we teach more than what may be listed in the district and state standards. All of us have settled disagreements between students on the playground, helped someone apologize, or given a student a hug after she shared materials with a peer. The Friendship Workshop concept is not a brand-new solution to building a caring community. It is not a quick fix for the struggles young children can have adjusting to a school community. And it is not just another program administrators want you to fit in to your already jam-packed and demanding schedules.

Friendship Workshop is a conscious approach to helping children identify and regulate their emotions so they can make choices that support their relationships and their schooling. It is a fresh way of observing students and using their actions to drive your teaching. It reframes how you react to their behaviors in order to support the literacy work you are already teaching. Friendship Workshop is a means for mindfully being with your students and building a caring, supportive community that learns and grows together.

Chapter 1

THE LANGUAGE OF LEARNING

D riving home from the very first grade-level meeting about literacy goals for the new school year, I felt completely overwhelmed. The enormous number of skills I was supposed to cover in nine months was daunting! Phonics, comprehension, punctuation, compare and contrast, high-frequency words, plurals, DRA Level 4—how would I get my kindergartners to research and write a nonfiction piece with captions, detailed descriptions, and question marks by the end of the year?

I turned into my driveway and told myself that working as a Starbucks barista might not be so bad. And then I remembered Nestor. Several years ago Nestor came to my kindergarten class one week after school had started. His family had just moved to Virginia from Guatemala and he had never been to a school, had never spoken or heard English, and was terrified of joining our classroom. He would stand at the door, clinging to his mom's leg and sobbing, "Pero ella no habla espanol, mami!" ("But she doesn't speak any Spanish, Mommy!"). Nestor found me as overwhelming as I found the new curriculum demands.

That year seventeen of my twenty-one students didn't know any letters of the alphabet. Twelve of them did not speak English as their first language. Nine of them were living below the poverty level, and the only meals they got were breakfast and lunch at school. Like Nestor, I wanted to cling to someone and sob, "My students need to play, feel safe, and make friends first!" (Figure 1.1 shows Margaret and Salma playing well together during indoor recess.)

Figure 1.1
Margaret and Salma say "Good game—thanks for playing with me!" when cleaning up.

At home I made a cup of hot tea, took a deep breath, and began breaking down the curriculum by looking at it as a yearlong continuum project. I asked myself, what is the real purpose of Reading and Writing Workshop? What are the big ideas in the standards for five-year-olds? What is it that I want my students to be able to do by June?

I thought about the true purpose of reading and writing, which is to communicate and connect. Directions for my favorite lasagna; a letter from my son, who was at boot camp; or a poem read at my friend's memorial service—these all communicate ideas and connect me to my life. The heart of communication is understanding. My son's letter let me understand that although basic training was hard, he was doing okay: "I know I can get through this with everyone sending cards to me all the time." The recipe directions taught me that the secret to yummy lasagna was placing garlic slices between the sheets of pasta. And the poem "Do Not Stand by My Grave and Weep" by Mary Elizabeth Frye allowed me to understand that my grief could be a celebration too.

As I continued unraveling these thoughts, I realized that to understand (or be understood) we need language. All kinds of language: oral language, written language, social language, and emotional language. Aha! *That's* my purpose in teaching Reading and Writing Workshop: to develop my students' capacity to use and understand these languages so they can communicate their ideas clearly and connect to one another.

It was then that a stronger memory of Nestor flashed before me. It was early March, six months after Nestor had moved to America, and my class was learning directional words. I took photographs of the children on the playground going across the bridge, standing next to the slide or behind the bench, and so on. Suddenly I heard Everett shout, "Ms. Buckley! Look at Nestor!" I glanced over to where Everett was pointing and there was Nestor on the monkey bars. Well, not exactly *on* the monkey bars.

"Nestor, what are you doing?" I asked him.

"I go *through* monkey bars, right?!" he said.

And sure enough, Nestor had wiggled himself through the tiny blue rings and lay there like a guinea pig in a maze! The grin on his face said it all. He understood the lesson, had the language to communicate his idea, and was thoroughly connecting with his friends. Developing Nestor's language through academic and social interactions over time had helped him feel confident enough to share his ideas and extend his own learning through play (see Figure 1.2).

Figure 1.2

Nestor demonstrates his understanding of the word *through* by squeezing himself through the monkey bars.

GETTING READY TO LEARN

Although there is no official definition of school readiness, many studies have found that traits such as controlling impulses, handling transitions, and cooperating with peers are strong predictors of academic success in later years. Children who live in poverty or come from language-poor backgrounds often have limited exposure to these crucial language skills. In their groundbreaking study of how the daily exchanges between a parent and child shape language and vocabulary knowledge, researchers Betty Hart and Todd Risley (1995) found that by age four, children from high-income families were exposed to thirty million more words than children from families on welfare. In follow-up studies, Hart and Risley revealed that the family exchanges had a significant bearing on children's performance in school, particularly in language development and reading comprehension. In addition to the thirty-million-word gap, children from poor families may also have much narrower conversations with parents and more negative reinforcement. For example, children from low-income families on average hear two discouraging words for every one encouraging word, whereas children from professional families hear six encouragements for every one discouragement (Hart and Risley 2003).

Think of the impact that pattern would have on your daily teaching—being reprimanded two times before hearing praise! The comparison to our professional lives gives me a better understanding of why some of my students don't ask questions directly and don't let me know when they are confused. It may be that they have not yet learned how to question and it may also be that they have been reprimanded for questioning. How many of us would remain silent if we expected harshness instead of clarity in response to our questions?

Students from language-deficient homes also typically lack experience with conversational skills that enable them to participate fully in our classroom exchanges. Their limited exposure to courteous conversations and open discussions may cause them to behave rudely or belligerently when confronted with unfamiliar dialogue and questions. Research shows that the conversations they tend to hear at home in their preschool years are often directive, close-ended, limiting, and unimaginative. The talk is about the immediate concerns of the moment: what to wear, what to eat, what is allowed or not allowed. These conversations rarely extend into future possibilities or wonderings. Directive and dictating language leaves children with a very concrete language base, which in turn can make understanding the abstract, decontextualized language of school threatening and intimidating (Roseberry-McKibbin 2012).

In a typical Reading or Writing Workshop, for example, students may be instructed to recall a past event, visualize specific details, and then employ the complicated and sophisticated rules of the English language. That is an enormous and daunting task for many young students, but especially for those with limited language skills.

Such weaknesses are not solely the domain of students from lower-income families. For example, our classrooms are becoming more diverse every year, with an increasing number of students who are learning English as their second language. As they access this new vernacular, students typically pass through five stages, as originally explained by linguist Stephen Krashen (1988). In the pre- and early-production stages of second-language acquisition, students are often hesitant to risk speaking openly in a group. Without a solid understanding of how to communicate respectfully and politely, they can feel worried, excluded, or fearful. To counteract anxiety and build a strong foundation for learning, teachers must establish a classroom environment that includes clear instructions, repeated practice, and playful exchanges (Moses Guccione 2012).

MANAGING CHANGE

As adults, we have a naive notion that childhood is carefree and easy. Children don't have to worry about health insurance or car payments or groceries. They play tag and take baths and have stories read to them before bed. But as Georgia Witkin, the director of the Mount Sinai School of Medicine Stress Research Program, writes in her book *Kid Stress* (1999), "It can't be, because all change is stressful (even good change) and young people's lives are filled with change" (14).

Teaching students to manage change is one of the most important parts of our job as educators in the primary grades. You probably won't find that task written in state or national standards and curriculum guides or hear the topic discussed in the faculty lounge at staff meetings, yet it is as vital to learning as reading and writing. Children who do not learn how to self-regulate their behaviors to respond appropriately to others' needs and demands and to navigate the slippery slope of transitions will likely fall behind in school and struggle throughout their lives. We must carefully cultivate their social and emotional intelligence just as we prime their academic growth.

C. Cybele Raver and Jane Knitzer from the National Center for Children in Poverty tell us, "Across a range of studies, the emotional, social, and behavioral competence of young children—such as higher levels of self-control and lower levels of acting out—predict their academic performance in first grade, over and above their cognitive skills and family backgrounds" (2002, 3).

In Friendship Workshop I address those social and emotional behaviors by connecting what I see my students doing and saying during independent work times with my insights about their developmental needs. I create a path to learning using their lives and emotions. Our conversations and discussions during Friendship Workshop help us reach academic standards; they don't pull us away from those goals. By understanding one another—orally and socially at first, then using those community-building exchanges to strengthen the skills of reading and writing—we experience the joys of communicating, understanding, and connecting to one another.

Chapter 2

TEACHING STUDENTS SELF-REGULATION SKILLS

As an experienced primary grades teacher, I know how to explicitly introduce and reinforce appropriate social interactions throughout the school day and school year. But when I was a new teacher, I didn't realize how crucial social and emotional learning were to a child's intellectual development or to the positive classroom culture I tried to maintain.

I vividly remember one day in my second year of teaching. I was sitting next to Mario during Writing Workshop. Two hours before, he had shoved a chair with such anger that both of us trembled afterward. At the time, he had been working at the science table, experimenting with sink and float objects. He was vigorous in his exploration and had to be reminded to keep the water inside the table.

His classmates complained (whined, really) that he was hogging all the funnels, and I noticed he used his elbows deftly to keep his classmates away from his side of the table. When time was up and his turn was over, Mario pretended not to hear the chime. He brushed off his classmates' reminders and shouted, "No!" as he propelled a chair forward with both hands. It knocked into the big book stand, which toppled over and hit me in the shins. It seemed as if the entire class froze and stopped breathing for a second.

In the ten steps it took me to reach Mario, I was able to look in his eyes. I did not see the typical wide-eyed stare that comes with the fear of being reprimanded, nor did I see the teary-eyed look of remorse. The look I saw was more defiant, as if challenging me to confront him. I took several deep breaths and sent Mario to the classroom next door.

This was not Mario's first emotional outburst, so we both knew the drill. He went to our buddy room for five minutes, giving both of us time to calm down. While Mario drew a picture of what he had done to upset the class, I gathered the other children together and we shared ideas about what Mario could have said instead of shoving the chair. We acknowledged the tension that he had created, responded with positive actions, and reinforced my intention of showing that Mario was kind; it was his *action* that was unkind.

After an appropriate discussion and break time, Mario rejoined us. When he sat down at the small rectangular writing table, he began working on his story about his older brother's new car. Earlier he had painstakingly drawn his brother's car and was going to color it blue when he finished his writing. Now he was struggling to sound out the word *brother*. Although he knew the procedure for sounding out words, he could identify only twelve letters of the alphabet and write just seven letters. The literacy challenge of connecting the sounds to the letter symbols was difficult for Mario, and so was Jessica's request that he share the blue crayon so she could color her picture. Mario was writing with a black felt-tip pen but clutched the blue crayon in his left hand.

In that moment I saw that Mario could focus either on sounding out the word (the literacy skill) or on sharing the blue crayon (the social skill), but he could not do both things at the same time. It was not that Mario lacked the ability to perform both skills; he was bright and energetic and learned quickly. Even so, his underdeveloped social and emotional learning was blocking his academic progress.

HOW THE BRAIN REACTS TO STRESS

When faced with a perceived threat, the human brain sets off signals to the nervous system: Do we need to fight or run? Do we need adrenaline for more energy? Our heart rate accelerates and blood sugar levels rise to help muscles work efficiently. The stress message also travels to the hormonal system, which triggers the emotional center. Long after a stressful situation, our hearts still pound and the worry remains. If these changes in the body's systems continue over time, they begin to impact the brain's normal functioning. The stress reduces the brain's ability to retain working memory while heightening the emotions. Simply stated, stress blocks our capacity to hold on to factual information while it increases the emotional sensations of fear, worry, and anxiety (The Franklin Institute 2004).

I remember the time my son went away for the weekend and accidentally took my key chain. I panicked and my thoughts raced: How will I get to work? I need to leave now to avoid traffic! My instructional assistant is out, and I need to set up the room! Should I call for a substitute?

While searching for a spare set of keys, I called a colleague, who drove twenty minutes out of her way to get me. Just as she pulled onto my street, I spied something by the back door: the valet key from the car dealer, with a big Saturn logo that was plain to see. In my stressed-out state, I had not seen the logical choice. My emotions took over.

This was not a life-or-death stress situation, of course, but my body sent the same stress signals I might feel when lost in a dark alley at night. For our students, what seem to us to be trivial or even illogical stresses can sometimes create similar sensations of pounding hearts and amplified energy. Whether they are trying to find a seat away from the big kids on the bus or waiting to get chosen for a team, children experience stresses that can inhibit their ability to process other information and make good choices.

Knowing how to handle these pressures and small injustices is an essential tool for learning. Self-regulation, also called executive functioning, impacts social, emotional, and cognitive development. Throughout the school day our classroom tasks require students to pay attention, cooperate with their peers, recall new information, and link it to previous learning—a multitude of processing skills that depend on a healthy state of mind.

WHAT MARIO TAUGHT HIS TEACHER

I thought about, worried about, and cried about Mario all year. I read book after book on child development, incessantly consulted the counselors, and worked with Mario one-on-one every chance I could. We talked about what it felt like to be angry and practiced specific sentences to use when he was feeling that way.

We started with just a deep growl instead of shouting and progressed to being able to say, "I am angry right now!" We learned ways to calm down and which friend would walk around the soccer field with him.

I also began observing Mario outside the classroom, which enabled me to see him in different situations and in different moods. I started staying in the classroom when the art and music teachers came, watched him on the playground, and stopped by the after-school program for a few minutes at a time. I saw that Mario was engaged and participated appropriately during music class. He waited patiently for a turn at the Wii game after school. During dismissal, he always found his kindergarten cousin and gave him a hug. I realized that Mario could be quiet, helpful, and tender. I am ashamed to admit that I had been caught in a vicious cycle of thinking that Mario was only capable of negative behaviors.

As I began to reflect on when his bad behaviors occurred as opposed to what the bad behaviors were, I identified a common catalyst—Mario often felt out of control. The water table incident was a typical reaction when he had to stop an activity he liked. If he had to clean up the paint set before he had colored his drawing of the sky, if he had to share materials with more than one person, or if he had to copy a worksheet template without any creative choices, Mario's temper flared. He would lash out at his peers, defy authority, and work himself into emotional and physical distress.

I wondered how I could better prepare him for transitions, provide consistent structures, and offer some options that suited his learning preferences. I had always given my students a five-minute warning before we switched activities, but I started giving Mario a ten-minute check-in and an array of other strategies designed to let him feel in charge.

- I might give him two options: "You can stay here at the math games, or would you like the last ten minutes at the magnet station?"

- I might offer to help him: "You have the sky and the snowman left to paint. Is there anything I can help with?"

- I might explicitly state what was possible: "You and Nhi won't have time to finish the book on tape. When the timer rings, use this sticky note to mark your place for tomorrow."

I also bought a pencil case and filled it with crayons, pencils, black pens, and glue sticks. I kept it by the front easel, so Mario could get his own materials when he needed to. Making these adaptations encouraged me to shift my thinking about other routines in the classroom. I never expected students to make identical paper ants for our science mural, so why would I expect all students to emotionally act the same way? Mario's frustration at having to copy a template taught me to model several different ways to do a project and then to take the models down from view. This allowed all students to appreciate their own creativity, and no one felt compelled to match the teacher's response. Mario's impatience taught me to step back when I was feeling annoyed and to take three deep breaths to calm down. Because his outbursts hurt everyone, I discovered the importance of including the whole class in discussions about behavior. It was because of Mario that I started reflecting and searching for small deliberate actions that would support the social and emotional needs of my students.

PERSONAL TRANSFORMATION

When June rolled around during my second year of teaching, as I was preparing the end-of-the-year progress reports, I struggled with my assessment of Mario. He had made significant improvements in both his social and academic learning and had successfully passed most of the end-of-the-year tests. However, he rarely applied his knowledge or expanded his thinking beyond the itemized skill. I did not believe that Mario's low achievement was based on a learning disability but rather on his struggle with regulating his social and emotional moods. I had several long discussions with the school administrators, the counselors, and Mario's mom. We agreed to promote Mario to first grade and continue to address his social and emotional needs. I worked closely with his first-grade teacher. Although he still struggled, Mario did make progress, both socially and academically.

Several years later I was watching a group of fourth graders read with my kindergarten students. The pairs were spread out around the classroom, sitting on pillows and rugs and behind bookcases. Most students had their Song and Poetry folders out and were reciting in unison. I noticed, however, that two students were going beyond the expected partner reading. Jason and his buddy were using whiteboards to write the high-frequency words collected from Jason's book box. His buddy would read the word aloud and then Jason would write it on the board. When Jason got it right, his buddy gave him a high five and a "Way to go!" cheer. When Jason misspelled a word, his buddy would write it correctly and show it to Jason. Then Jason would try again and get it right. His buddy was thoughtful, kind, and patient. His buddy was Mario.

Had my interventions during kindergarten caused this shift in his behavior by the fourth grade? I would not be so bold as to claim that direct influence. Mario had a loving mother, a series of dedicated teachers, and the time to mature. But I do think my explicit teaching of the language of learning helped Mario begin to control his emotions and progress in school. More important, the process helped me understand the urgency and consequence of teaching social and emotional skills to my students.

THE "MISSING PIECE"

In 2012 the Collaborative for Academic, Social, and Emotional Learning (CASEL), the nation's leading organization in integrating social and emotional learning into our schools, commissioned a national teacher survey entitled "The Missing Piece." In it, they outline the academic and societal benefits of educational programs in schools that include explicit teachings of self-regulation skills. John Bridgeland, the report's coauthor, says, "Now we know those on the frontline—our teachers—agree that social and emotional learning is the missing piece to boost student outcomes and transform our schools" (Civic Enterprises et al. 2012).

Supporting students is what teachers do best. We have all made the decision to pause a lesson to help diffuse a disagreement at the computer station, or shifted a child's bad mood with a high five when he silently picked up someone else's coat off the floor, or helped a child apologize when the words seemed too scary to say. Teachers know self-regulation skills can make or break a classroom environment. Armed with research and resolve, we can now confidently address the fuller dimensions of learning, making instructional and interpersonal choices that are vital for children's social, emotional, and academic development.

Studies show that teaching children to address their social and emotional needs is an effective way to improve their academic achievement. As Gould and Knight write, "To prevent academic failure, students need encouragement and explicit instruction in these areas" (2009).

The following chapters present ways to structure this multifaceted instruction, blending literacy lessons with life lessons and oral language practice that enables young students to confidently navigate school. As I did with Mario, I offer suggestions and choices, not absolutes. Every class is unique, and your circumstances may differ from mine. What we have in common is a desire to help our students succeed.

Self-Regulating:
Give a brain break &
tell why we're doing it.

Choices - expectation stays
the same - "Are you going
to do the writing @ your
desk or over here?"

"A game table" - positive spot
to work.

Chapter 3

THE FRIENDSHIP WORKSHOP FORMAT

There is a poster in the multiage classroom at Happy Medium School in Seattle that says, "Let's talk. Let's all talk. What we don't talk about hurts us all" (Teaching Tolerance Project 1997, 2). I teach Friendship Workshop specifically because *not* talking about our hurts and mistakes openly and honestly sends a hidden message of negativity and disapproval. On the other hand, an open and sincere dialogue sends the caring message of acceptance and forgiveness.

The format for Reading, Writing, or Math Workshop consists of a whole-group mini-lesson on a specific topic followed by a period of group discussion and instruction. The students then spread out to practice while the teacher works with specific groups. The workshop finishes with the students sharing their work and reflecting on their new learning.

Friendship Workshop follows this same format. The mini-lesson might consist of sharing a read-aloud or looking at a photograph or watching a short video clip. The focus is always on one specific social or emotional skill (although the lessons and discussions tend to blend into one another). Whenever possible, I use our daily interactions as examples so the lessons become personal and authentic. This enables our discussions to be concrete and straightforward, which encourages honesty when we admit our mistakes and sincerity when we apologize.

The discussion time is for students to share their experiences in our safe circle. Our safe circle looks the same as Morning Meetings and mini-lessons. The difference is that I am less the teacher and more an equal member of the group. I purposefully admit mistakes and openly apologize. It may be something small: "Friends, I am sorry we cannot finish our paintings today. I made a mistake and forgot to sign up for the art room. Another class is already using it." When I frame my failings as mistakes, the students begin to see that making mistakes is normal and apologizing can be easy.

One time a bigger event required me to be brutally honest with myself as well as the class. Jack was exceptionally "energetic" one day and I was at my limit. A group of teachers was coming to observe our science lesson and Jack had knocked over all the plantings, torn the science poster we had made, and created a mud puddle in his effort to clean up the soil. There was nothing left of my lesson—or my patience. I raised my voice, told Jack to sit in a chair, and said, "DO NOT MOVE because you've made enough of a mess already." (Not my proudest moment; still stings.)

I was so focused on making a good impression on the visiting teachers that I had forgotten the children would be feeling excited too. I had let my focus shift from the students being scientists to the class being my showpiece. Ouch. In our Friendship Workshop the next day I put aside the lesson on interrupting politely and told the class about my feelings.

"Yesterday I was very excited to have the teachers from Japan coming to visit our room for our science lesson. I wanted everything to go just right. When Jack tried to help and things got messy I got very frustrated, didn't I?" (Heads nodded vigorously; clearly Jack wasn't the only one I had hurt.) "Well, I made a terrible mistake. I got mad at Jack and raised my voice. I made him feel like he made the mess on purpose. I know he was trying to help, but in the moment I was really annoyed."

I had apologized to Jack the day before, but because I remembered reading a relevant quote somewhere ("A private apology will never make up for a public humiliation"), I turned directly to Jack. "Jack, you are always so helpful and I know you wanted things to go right yesterday too. I am sorry I took my frustration out on you. I shouldn't have raised my voice at you. I am sorry I hurt you." Jack, with his chunky cheek dimple tugging at my heart, said, "It's okay, Ms. Buckley. I forgive you," and he wrapped me in a hug. Oh, the lessons these little ones give us! (See Figure 3.1 for Jack's beautiful smile.)

Figure 3.1
Jack's dimples melted my
heart every time!

TARGETING OUR EMOTIONS

Talking honestly requires us to reveal our mistakes or lack of knowledge and risk embarrassment. Without trust, exchanging math ideas, taking risks in art, or adapting to a schedule change can feel dangerous. Without trust, disagreements can carry over from one day to another and learning can shut down. Trusting relationships foster the necessary dialogues that enable us to learn from one another. We feel connected and accepted and safe.

During our discussion time, if our topic is "interrupting politely," students might tell of times when they got in trouble with their parents for being rude and how it felt to be scolded. Other students will share their similar tales of misbehavior. These connections reveal that we have all felt frustration and have also caused frustration for others. The message I want to send is that we all make mistakes and must learn to forgive one another.

After our conversation, we do an activity to highlight the targeted emotion. It might be drawing or coloring, a group art project, or a think-pair-share activity. My real purpose is to create time for the children to chat about their personal experiences (see Figure 3.2). Most activities are very basic and simple and require little prep work. Occasionally we will extend our learning through activities the children initiate. For example, we have made books about emotions, posters illustrating "How to Wait," and photo collages of our apologies, all stemming from the students' needs and ideas. During the activities, children casually converse about how the particular emotion has shown up in their own lives and I wander the classroom and listen to their talk. I am always struck by their powerful insights. I use this time to work one-on-one

Figure 3.2
Jaida and Sydney work together.

with selected students, emphasizing how our emotions are normal, temporary, and changeable states of mind.

In Friendship Workshop the social component is the work students do or show outwardly while interacting with others. It may be a specific phrase or gesture they use with one another. It may be learning when to plan with a peer and when to choose a quiet spot to work alone. The emotional component is the metacognitive work the children do, including developing self-awareness skills that enable them to choose their actions wisely. It may be taking three deep breaths to calm down before speaking or it may be allowing a friend to take the first cupcake. These components blend seamlessly together to enhance the literacy lessons that make up so much of the curriculum in the primary grades.

All teachers have had students who get hyperfocused on an activity. In my classroom, Adam loved the computer math game called Coin Critters. He chose it at math centers, at free time, and during indoor recess. He became distraught when he couldn't play it, and once when it was his turn Adam actually shoved another student out of the chair because he felt she was taking too long to switch centers. "I'm losing time," he would cry. Basic lessons on taking turns, checking the chart for his turn, and waiting patiently were not working for Adam.

When we did our activity on waiting patiently, and most students drew "How to Wait" pictures of singing to themselves or counting to one hundred in their heads, I helped Adam create a chart to use when he had to wait for the computer game. As Adam and I cut and pasted the icons on his chart, I asked him if he played better when he was upset or when he was calm. What was different when he was upset and when he was in control? I told him he was strong enough to keep himself calm while he waited. Just as he did when he played Coin Critters, I told him, he had choices. He could choose to get upset *or* he could choose to use the chart to stay peaceful and safe. I wanted to shift his state of mind from thinking that being upset was out of his control to realizing he had an option and a solution to feel better.

ROLE-PLAYING OUR FEELINGS

Other lessons might involve the class role-playing a situation to help internalize the lessons. I carefully orchestrate these scenes so that the message of the lesson remains loud and clear. I perform the misdeed for the first few scenes to show how to be in control and I always ask permission from the "victim" before starting. I overexaggerate my actions so there is a light tone to the situation but reinforce during the reflection time that hurting someone's feelings or body is a serious matter.

I learned the importance of choosing which students to role-play when I asked Jesus to be one of our class actors. Jesus was a stocky first grader who was quite a bit larger than his classmates. He had the sweetest smile and would offer to help at a moment's notice, but he also had a tendency to knock over the crayon bin, drop and trip on his sweatshirt, or spill his Goldfish crackers at least once a day. As an adult (and parent), I could see Jesus hadn't grown into his body yet and wasn't aware of where his personal space ended and someone else's started. His classmates were less understanding. So I decided to plan a lesson about being peaceful when someone bumps you.

I invited several students to pretend to stand in the lunch line with me. I gave Rabia a lunch tray and instructed her to quietly hum a song to herself as she rocked back and forth. When she accidentally bumped into me, I turned around and said, "Hey! Quit hitting me!" The class giggled.

"Let me try that again," I said. Rabia hummed and bumped me again. "Ow! Ms. Buckley! She hit me!" I said, imitating a student's outburst. The class laughed and told me that wasn't a good response.

"One more try," I said. Rabia did her part again and I went for the standard response, "Owwwwwww! Stooooop iiiiiit!," which took a full twenty seconds to say because I dragged it out in that high-pitched whine we teachers know so well. After the giggles subsided we discussed how apologizing feels nicer for everyone and decided to act out the scene again in the proper way using our phrase, "I'm sorry. It was an accident. Are you okay?"

I invited Jesus to be the "bumper" this time. He pretended to be running on the playground and knocked into Basit harder than necessary. Basit's face and voice let us know he was not pretending. "Hey, that hurt," he said, and Jesus responded without thinking. "It wasn't my fault!" he shouted. The class stopped and looked at me for guidance. I looked at Jesus as he mumbled in a quiet voice, "Well, it wasn't."

I realized this lesson was really hard for Jesus. As much as I knew he accidentally bumped into things, I had never put myself in his place. It often *isn't* his fault, yet the annoyed responses from his peers or from me always made apologizing harder for him. He didn't feel safe enough to admit hurting someone. I wanted to help Jesus know that apologizing can be hard but, like learning to read or subtract, we do our best and help one another.

"You're right, Jesus," I said. "I'm so excited you said that! It wasn't your fault—that's exactly what an accident is. But sometimes when a friend yells at us or uses a nasty tone we want to be nasty back, don't we? But, Jesus, how are you feeling now?"

"Bad."

"Yeah, I can tell. So being nasty back to Basit didn't fix the problem, did it? Basit, how do you feel?"

"Mad."

"I bet. Now both of you feel cruddy. When we apologize it means we want our friend to feel better. Jesus, did you mean to hurt Basit? No, you didn't. No one in our room ever means to hurt someone. It was an accident and we all cause them. When we apologize we are saying, 'I like you and I want to use my strong heart to help you feel better.' Do you friends want to try again and use the words we've been practicing?"

Jesus and Basit reenacted the playground scene, and this time Jesus said the "I'm sorry" phrase. Basit replied, "Yep, I'm okay. Thanks, Jesus."

I kept a close eye on Jesus during the next few days and found those teachable moments where he could practice apologizing in our safe and caring community.

THE WEEKLY SCHEDULE

My Friendship Workshop is a weekly, thirty-minute session that is a regular part of school. Just as I do for music class or P.E., I use a schedule card with an icon of children holding hands to establish a set time and day for our workshop. This consistent visual reminder is vital to help students internalize that these lessons are as important as what they might do during Reading Workshop or science centers. Sometimes I use the time for a short review lesson, or I might develop the theme into a longer lesson if the topic is particularly relevant to the children. The key is returning to the workshop every week and planning and reflecting on the content with the same thoughtful attention that I give to reading records or math notebooks.

For the first month of school, Friendship Workshop happens every day for fifteen minutes. I am trying to build the children's stamina for incorporating our community-building lessons as I also reinforce the consistency of the practice. These short sessions usually consist of silly songs or simple read-alouds. I do not give a lesson or discuss sensitive issues yet because I want to set the tone for the rest of the year without overwhelming the children.

Over time the needs of the class and the specific situations will dictate our lessons, but the first weeks lay the foundation for empathy and acceptance so there is a need for a more teacher-directed tone to the lessons. I want my students to know that even when things are hard, there will always be comfort, kindness, joy, and safety in our classroom. The first song we share is simple (see Figure 3.3):

> *I am special.*
> *I am special.*
> *Look at me.*
> *You will see.*
> *Someone very special.*
> *Someone very special.*
> *It is me.*
> *It is me.*

Figure 3.3
During the first week of school we make self-portraits to accompany our "I Am Special" song.

We create a self-portrait poster of what makes each one of us special. Emma Ly has two parts to her name, Marcos has lost a tooth, Rabia and Sulimaan can speak both English and Urdu. Hearing and understanding that we are all fundamentally special is an important aspect of Friendship Workshop. This is not the same kind of activity as a generic "Johnny likes basketball" sharing. Rather, I want the children to identify their unique qualities. I believe it is important for the children to separate the things *they have* from *who they are*. This is the beginning of empathy and deep connections.

As the children share what makes them special, I guide them past the examples that are based on materialistic things. For example, when Josue said he was special because he had a Wii game at home, I shifted his thinking away from his prized physical possessions.

"That is exciting, Josue," I said. "I've played the Wii bowling game. It was fun. What games do you have?"

"I have bowling, but it's boring. Mario Kart, Michael Jackson—that's my favorite. The music is cool."

Several classmates exclaimed that they played Michael Jackson after school at SACC (School Age Child Care) and they liked it, too.

"Josue, I'm thinking that maybe it's not the Wii that makes you special, because a few of your friends have the game too. Which part of the Michael Jackson game makes you feel special?"

"The moonwalk," he said. "It took me a while to learn but now I can do it really good. Want to see?"

He shared an impromptu lesson, and Josue added his fancy dance skills to his poster. At recess, I noticed Josue giving his classmates private dance lessons.

We use the "I Am Special" song to make other posters during the first weeks of school. Here are some ideas:

What makes me feel strong?

I can help . . .

I feel safe when . . .

It feels nice when someone . . .

The song quickly becomes a soothing background hum that I hear as we clean up centers, line up in the cafeteria, and walk out to dismissal. I've seen grins on parents' faces when their children teach them the song and proudly explain what makes them so special. When my students leave school trusting that I find them special, then teaching becomes easier and more enjoyable for all of us.

CORE SOCIAL AND EMOTIONAL SKILLS

Over the years, as I designed and redesigned Friendship Workshop, I kept notes on the social and emotional skills that were the most troublesome for my students. Some years I had a pack of criers, or a set of hitters, or other years a happy-go-lucky group that needed help listening and working together. Each year the specific dynamics of my class changed, but I began to see a core set of social and emotional skills that students need to successfully navigate the complexities of becoming a school classroom community. These include the following:

- Getting Along: Being Part of a Group

- Empathy

- Kindness

- Peacefulness

- Responsibility

- Self-Control

- Perseverance

- Giving and Getting Feedback

Figure 3.4 lists the topics and some related resources that we can use to develop these themes in literacy lessons.

Figure 3.4

Friendship Workshop Themes and Related Resources

THEME	USEFUL RESOURCES
Getting Along: Being Part of a Group	*The Colors of Us*—Karen Katz *It's Okay to Be Different*—Todd Parr *Life in a Crowded Place: Making a Learning Community*—Ralph Peterson
Empathy	*The Recess Queen*—Alexis O'Neill *The Other Side*—Jacqueline Woodson *The Compassionate Classroom: Relationship Based Teaching and Learning*—Sura Hart and Victoria Kindle Hodson
Kindness	*One*—Kathryn Otoshi *Those Shoes*—Maribeth Boelts *Glenna's Seeds*—Nancy Edwards *Starting Small*—Teaching Tolerance Project (book and DVD)
Peacefulness	*Wangari's Trees of Peace: A True Story from Africa*—Jeanette Winter *All the World*—Liz Garton Scanlon *The Power of Our Words: Teacher Language That Helps Children Learn*—Paula Denton

continued

Responsibility	*Mr. Peabody's Apples*—Madonna *Down the Road*—Alice Schertle *Choosing to Learn: Ownership and Responsibility in a Primary Multiage Classroom*—Penelle Chase and Jane Doan
Self-Control	*Sit-In: How Four Friends Stood Up by Sitting Down*—Andrea Davis Pinkney *When Sophie Gets Angry—Really Really Angry . . .*—Molly Bang *Choice Words: How Our Language Affects Children's Learning*—Peter Johnston
Perseverance	*The Most Magnificent Thing*—Ashley Spires *Brave Irene*—William Steig *Terrific*—Jon Agee *How Children Succeed: Grit, Curiosity, and the Hidden Power of Character*—Paul Tough
Giving and Getting Feedback	*Go Dog. Go!*—P. D. Eastman *Don't Forget to Share: The Crucial Last Step in the Writing Workshop*—Leah Mermelstein

To determine the needs of my students and develop the lessons that will support their social and emotional learning, I ask myself a series of questions about their behaviors and reflect on specific ways that I can guide their growth. Chapters 5–11 include charts that outline the typical questions I ask, the possible needs students might have, and some specific actions to implement. Here I summarize how each social and emotional skill shows up in my classroom and the importance of explicitly teaching these skills to my young students.

Being Part of a Group

As adults, we have been in large groups of people dozens of times and might take for granted the intricate coping mechanisms we use to adjust. We move our bodies to create personal space, we lower our voices in small groups, we wait for things to be handed out, and we trust we will get what we need. These reactions do not come naturally to young children, however. Learning to function within a large school family is an important step for creating an effective classroom community.

Empathy

Empathy is the basis of all my teaching. I deeply believe that connecting to others in a kind and honest way creates a class that functions smoothly, learns enthusiastically, and supports all learners. For students in the primary grades, who are at a highly egotistical developmental stage, understanding another's needs and interests can be difficult, yet it is a vital cog in the learning cycle. We first identify a personal inner sense of well-being, learning to be empathetic to ourselves. From that kindness, we nurture a healthy self-concept, making it easier to relate to and empathize with others.

Kindness

In the early weeks of school, students are just learning to move and control their bodies in the small space of the classroom. Nudges, pokes, and brushes happen frequently, and it's not always clear to young children if the contact was unintentional or a personal violation. In Friendship Workshop we discuss the terms *accident* and *on purpose*. We brainstorm different types of accidents, such as spilling milk and wrecking the car. A baby's diaper accident always gets mentioned! We write down the types of things we do on purpose (eat, hang up our coats, brush our teeth). I steer the conversation to the playground and we talk about what we do on purpose when we are at recess. What kind of accidents can happen on the playground?

When we discuss kindness we also discuss our emotions. Not just "happy to be in school" emotions but the very, very real and sticky emotions of jealousy, anxiety, self-doubt, and loss. The books *One* by Kathyrn Otoshi and *The Recess Queen* by Alexis O'Neill are powerful examples of these emotions and always bring us closer together as a class. Five-year-olds are very astute and have genuinely struggled with the deep feelings these books highlight: the sadness of being picked on, the fear of someone bigger, and the courage of following our hearts to do what's right. Purposely setting aside time and space to teach children that these "big emotions" are normal permits students to become vulnerable and open their hearts to one another.

Every year, from the discussions of these books, some students take the risk to admit that they are bullies. As a class we all know it; we are the ones suffering from their intimidation tactics. But being honest and laying the cards on the table, so to speak, shifts the situation back into balance. We learn we all make mistakes and we all can be forgiven. This translates into fewer snide comments when someone shares a different math answer or when someone's drawing looks unusual.

Peacefulness

With the constant demands of learning standards and high-stakes assessments, teachers may lose sight of the experiences and skills that students need to be *able* to learn. For me, the most important benchmark is a student's capacity to feel safe, calm, and peaceful.

We tend to assume, for example, that our young students know what it means to feel good. Ask them when they feel happy and they might say, "When my mom buys me presents" or "When we go to McDonald's." When I ask my students what it *feels* like to be happy, many cannot identify the sensation. I realized that they often used *not* when defining happiness, as in "When I'm not crying" or "When my mom isn't yelling" or "When I'm not in trouble." If I can help them notice and explicitly define what happiness feels like, I believe they will be more patient with themselves and more empathetic to their peers.

Responsibility

Making mistakes is an inevitable part of learning, of being human. Choosing to be responsible for them is a skill that must be explicitly taught, however. When students feel safe to admit their mistakes and be gently forgiven for them, they become trustful, and respect flourishes in our classroom community. Likewise, when we feel secure emotionally we can stretch ourselves educationally by being willing to take risks in learning.

When students regularly identify their own emotional states and accept responsibility for the classroom environment, they begin learning how to take care of the group. They share jobs, offer help, and acknowledge mistakes. Together we learn the components of a conversation: the give and take of information, the back and forth of taking turns, and the joint effort that is required to understand each other.

Self-Control

Continuing our work on recognizing emotions, we start to talk about self-control. We now know what it means to be peaceful and what our faces and bodies feel like when we are calm and content. Self-control teaches us to notice how our bodies feel; our shoulders may rise or our hands may clench when we feel frustrated. It means calming ourselves down through focused breathing or other relaxing techniques. We learn to respond to a friend's body language as a form of self-control; if their face is angry we can move away to give them some alone time. I help the students practice these self-control skills in silly ways. For example, I may notice Adolfo is very focused on trying to tie his shoe, so I will jokingly announce to the class that I think Adolfo might get frustrated and we can help him calm down.

"Let's take three deep breaths with Adolfo. Ready? Oh . . . that's good, I feel better now, don't you? Phewfers, that was close. It's a good thing we know how to calm down."

These silly moments create reference points for students when they need to calm down.

In addition, when they feel in control, it will be easier for them to support a friend who is frustrated at not being able to draw her picture "just right." As the curriculum expectations become harder, students may feel pressure or worried about their ability to keep up. It is essential that our sense of community and caring stay strong in order to support the new challenges in our learning.

Perseverance and Delayed Gratification

Research shows that preschool-age children who can persevere with difficult situations or delay gratification are better equipped as adolescents and adults both socially and academically (Shoda, Mischel, and Peake 1990). By contrast, children who have difficulty persevering through problematic situations or applying delayed gratification may come across as bossy or selfish. They often have not yet fully internalized an inner sense of peace and may feel they will be left out or lose out if they are not first. When children learn the tools of perseverance such as self-talk, self-distraction, or creating internal cognitive activities, they are able to postpone their immediate reactions (physical or emotional) and make choices that support their desired outcomes.

We learn how to interrupt politely when people are talking, control ourselves while waiting in the lunch line, and read to ourselves while ignoring distractions. We learn to pause and reevaluate a situation in order to determine the best course of action.

Giving and Getting Feedback

Giving and receiving feedback requires us to be kind, responsible, and accepting of different ideas—skills we develop all year long. We also must extend kindness to ourselves. In giving and receiving feedback, students learn to self-evaluate their reading and writing as they discuss the quality of their work. Not everything they draw or write will be great, and evaluating the work and not the person is an important concept to learn. We explore feeling satisfied with our work as well as not feeling proud of our work. We are reminded of our "self-talk" skill and practice silently, checking to see if our comments to a friend are helpful or hurtful.

During writing activities, students might look at their work and ask questions such as "Does it make sense?" and "Do my illustrations help the reader?" During math lessons, they might ask, "Was I clear in my explanation?" and "Does my work show every step in solving it?" I encourage the children to be specific and positive with their words and choose one thing to change or improve in their work. As they extend these lessons to conversations with classmates, they learn the importance of using phrases such as "Thanks for the idea" and "Maybe next time I'll try that."

THE SOCIAL-EMOTIONAL CONNECTIONS TO LEARNING

The social and emotional skills that frame Friendship Workshop become my affective curriculum. The themes create a learning environment that is rigorous, dynamic, and supportive. Each class has its own unique needs, and I mix and match the lessons as necessary.

The next chapter looks at how these social and emotional lessons prepare students for school and reinforce the literacy skills that are essential for all communication.

Chapter 4

EXTENDING FRIENDSHIP WORKSHOP TO LITERACY LESSONS

As a gymnastics coach, I always had students who wanted to do flips and aerials before they were ready. Flips are amazing feats and make people say, "Wow!" but there are dozens of smaller, less flashy skills that need to be refined first: sit-ups for abdominal strength, plyometrics for lift power, lunges to build leg muscles—all the repetitious and boring skills that can try children's patience.

I understood their desire to defy gravity, so every now and then I would physically carry my gymnasts through a flip. I did all the work: I lifted them, rotated them, and then landed them safely. They got to soar through the air, hear the cheers from their friends, and feel the excitement of being a "real" gymnast. I did this not just to see the delight on their faces but also so they could experience the sensations of flipping and imagine doing it on their own.

As a teacher, I have found that the same process works in Writing Workshop. Long before my students know all twenty-six letters and their corresponding sounds, before they are "ready" to write, I carry them through the skills and thrills of writing a book.

EXPERIENCING THE THRILL

Betzy was a native Spanish speaker, an only child who had no preschool experience. She recognized the letter *B* in her name but did not know how to form any letters. She did know three color names: red, blue, and purple. At the beginning of kindergarten all her drawings were swatches of these colors. No figures, no flowers, just scribbles of varying length and width.

One day I pulled my chair next to Betzy and talked with her. As I pointed to one of her scribbles I prompted, "This color is . . ."

"Blue!" Betzy answered while her blue crayon continued to dance across the page in a seemingly chaotic, patternless fashion.

"You are right. It is blue. Blue like things we can see. The blue sky, the blue chairs, Amner's blue shirt . . ."

"Sofia's shoes have lights," Betzy offered.

Hmm, I thought, maybe Betzy doesn't know blue after all. I decided to check where she was going with this.

"Sofia, can you come over here, please? Betzy says your shoes have lights."

Sofia promptly and proudly stomped her feet. Across the tops of her shoes were dazzling blue lights jumping this way and that—in a seemingly chaotic, patternless fashion!

"Betzy, you were right!" I said. "Sofia's shoes have fancy blue lights! Wow, I never noticed those before!"

A small smile leapt across Betzy's face and she showed me her next drawing—big curving scribbles of purple with three circular splotches of darker purple.

I leaned in close and said, "I know this color. It's your favorite, isn't it?"

Betzy nodded. "I like purple. I wear it every day."

"So you do," I said. "What else is purple? Grapes, our one hundred chart."

Betzy chimed in, "Jane Ritchie's headband is purple."

I called Jane Ritchie over, and sure enough, there was a curved purple headband with three flowers on one side.

"Betzy, you are a genius! You see so many colors in our room. Let's write a book to help our class learn their colors, okay?"

I asked Betzy to get the stapler and two more pieces of blank paper. I organized her book with a blank page for the cover, the blue page, the purple page, and a blank page for her yet-to-be-drawn red page.

"Let's start your book, Betzy. What should we say here?"

"Sofia's shoes has lights."

I repeated her phrase with one change: "Sofia's shoes have *blue* lights." Then I turned the page. "What should we say here?"

"Jane Ritchie's headband has flowers," Betzy said.

I repeated the sentence, with one change: "Jane Ritchie's headband has *purple* flowers."

"What color will go on this page?" I asked next.

"Red!" shouted Betzy.

"You got it, and what things do you know that are red?"

Betzy needed no prompting. "Samuel's backpack has Angry Birds!"

I glanced over to the cubbies and there was a big red Angry Bird icon on Samuel's backpack. Betzy and I read her book together and I left her to color a bright red blob—I mean, backpack.

There were no letters written or sounds articulated or fingers pointing to words, but Betzy got to feel the thrill of her words being repeated, her ideas being shared, her voice being heard. Like my gymnasts, I physically carried her through the steps of writing a book based on her interest, her knowledge, and her words. She got to feel the thrill of being an author (see Figure 4.1).

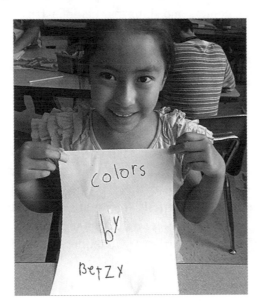

Figure 4.1
Betzy shows off her book cover.

THE DEVELOPMENT OF LITERACY WORKSHOPS

My Literacy Workshops are designed with that same sort of authenticity and thrill in mind, all year long. Building confidence, discovering possibilities, and learning content blend together rather seamlessly, so that the themes we learn in Friendship Workshop carry over to literacy lessons, and vice versa.

During the first six weeks of school, my goal is to create an environment that encourages students to feel connected to one another, feel safe to share ideas, and believe they are capable. We focus initially on the process of learning, not the products of understanding. I want students to come together as learners, not jump into memorizing facts. I want them to share questions, not limit themselves to the "right" answers. I seek to develop a desire—no, a need—to write because they feel compelled to share, to express themselves, to teach one another.

Much as I developed Friendship Workshop over the years, I developed Literacy Workshop through stages of reading this, trying that, and adapting almost everything. No one year looks exactly like the one before. I always build on what the students teach me and try to find ways to improve my craft. I do, however, start with a rough outline of the social and emotional skills that will support the literacy learning and help connect the curriculum to our lives (see Figure 4.2). Although the content and skills that I emphasize ebb and flow, the basic links are these:

1. Being Part of a Group and Empathy connect to Oral Storytelling and Presenting a Performance based on a favorite book.

As they learn to share their lives through oral storytelling, my students discover that they have something important to say. They become engrossed in making meaning, clarifying ideas, and being heard by an audience. The students read their stories in pairs, small groups, or to the whole class at the end of Writing Workshop. They learn to introduce themselves, tell their stories clearly, and answer questions thoughtfully. Toward the end of the unit we choose a favorite text and create a short retelling of the book. We visit buddy classrooms and delight in sharing our new storytelling skills. The students are

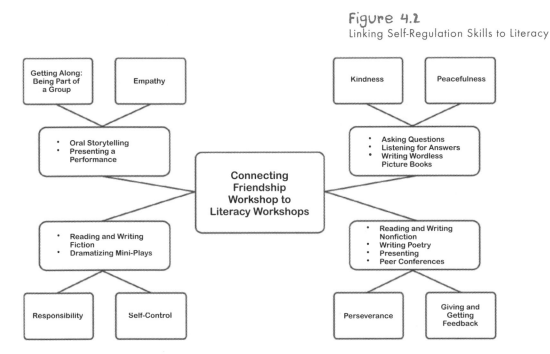

Figure 4.2
Linking Self-Regulation Skills to Literacy

free to change their stories often after the initial telling (which is also the very first editing and revising they do) without worrying about voice-print match, first-letter correspondence, or other conventions of the writing process. As a result, they become confident communicators who are eager to offer and receive suggestions.

During Writing Workshop we focus on sharing stories, listening to stories, and understanding stories. Writing Workshop is where we deepen our connections to one another and deepen our understanding of *why* we read and write.

2.   Kindness and Peacefulness connect to Asking Questions, Listening for Answers, and Writing Wordless Picture Books.

I don't want to let students develop bad habits in the rush to get them writing. Many teachers forget (or don't know) that handwriting involves much more than just fine-motor control. The skills that go into learning how to form letters support literacy, but many teachers rush to get stories down on paper. That is not my aim. Handwriting requires memory, focus, prediction, sequencing, estimation, patience, and specific knowledge of letter formation and sound correlation. Phewfers! If I allow time for my students to develop the skills of storytelling before requiring all those features, I believe when they actually record the work with letters and words, the process will be much more fluent, cohesive, and engaging.

Language comprehension, expressive language, reasoning, and memory are cognitive functions that get students ready to write (Marr, Windsor, and Cermak 2001). In the first months of school, I want to prime their brains for sharing stories in multiple ways. During Friendship Workshop and Writing Workshop, I give students ample opportunities to ask questions—politely—and listen to answers—thoughtfully—as peers share wordless picture books they have written to illustrate their oral stories. Practicing kindness and peacefulness as they do so develops their capacity to understand others, which is a vital part of literacy, whether recognizing character motivation in fiction or point of view in nonfiction writing. We continue to work on the conventions of writing such as recognizing and using high-frequency words and letter names and sounds during other parts of the school day.

3. <u>Responsibility and Self-Control</u> connect to <u>Reading and Writing Fiction</u> and <u>Dramatizing Mini-Plays</u> based on student stories.

Responsibility and self-control begin our formal writing of books. With a strong understanding of the beginning, middle, and end of plots and character development as well as the presentation and resolution of problems, students start writing fiction. We learn to have conversations about our work as we practice the responsibility skills of thinking before reacting and staying focused on one topic, and the self-control skills of waiting patiently and interrupting politely.

A true conversation is following another's thoughts and building meaning together. As writers, we want to be certain our stories make sense and engage the reader. We act responsibly when we recognize we don't understand something and ask for clarification.

4. <u>Perseverance</u> connects to <u>Reading and Writing Nonfiction</u> in pairs and <u>Presenting</u> work.

Perseverance is vital to lifelong learning. Nonfiction is a favorite genre for most students because they are naturally curious about the world around them. Although working in pairs is often not something they are naturally curious about, the shared learning helps expand previous lessons about kindness, patience, and self-control into our daily work. As students work together, they practice listening, respecting, and making deliberate choices based on what's best for the project and not just their selfish desires. Dr. Jill Gilkerson, a language research director at the Language Environment Analysis Foundation, writes, "Talk is powerful, but what's even more powerful is engaging a child in meaningful interactions—the 'give and take' that is so important to the social, emotional and cognitive development" (University of California–Los Angeles 2009).

5.   Giving and Getting Feedback connects to Writing Poetry and Peer Conferences.

Giving and receiving feedback is the culminating lesson of my school year. Poetry gives students the chance to express themselves in unique ways while honing their literacy skills of "snap" words, rhymes, punctuation, and other conventions of reading and writing, and giving and receiving feedback on their work builds on all the social lessons: being kind, being respectful, being part of a group, practicing empathy, and taking responsibility for their work. Students learn to accept that their grades reflect our effort as a group as well as their progress in learning the academic skills of revising, comprehending, fluency, expression, and so on. Feedback includes speaking confidently, and this brings students full circle: they are authors and scientists and poets who have a story to tell, a fact to teach, an emotion to share.

I HAVE SOMETHING TO SAY

If Betzy's experience with the "gymnastics thrill" of writing a book represents the beginning of the school year, Samuel's experience shows how the lessons in Friendship Workshop help students develop literacy confidence by the end of the year. It is late April now, and my kindergarten classroom is deep into Writing Workshop. Emma has made a makeshift desk in the reading corner and is sharing her story with the stuffed animals. Amner has planted himself right in front of the word wall for easy access to his friends' names. Marcos and Jessica are crammed next to each other, happily discussing their book about twisting the swings and flying like helicopters. Samuel, however, is classically avoiding work. He has searched the basket for just the right pencil, chatted with friends about recess, and used the bathroom. He heads to the water fountain for the second time when I interrupt him.

"Samuel, I noticed you didn't get any words down yesterday. What was tricky for you yesterday?" I ask.

Samuel is a Spanish speaker who did not attend preschool. He joined us in kindergarten five weeks after school started. He has difficulty with articulation as well as sequencing his thoughts. He has just qualified for speech services.

Samuel shrugs his shoulders and looks down at the ground, answering my question with indifference.

"I know some days it can be hard to get started," I say, trying a different approach. "When we look up at our Writing Workshop chart, what's number one?"

"I think about my story," he says.

"Right! Was it hard for you to think about your story yesterday?"

Samuel nods his head with a sad face.

"Would you like some help with that today?" I offer.

Samuel proceeds to say bits and pieces of sentences of what I think are random words at first. I repeat what I think he said, but Samuel is determined to correct me when I misunderstand.

"I see brown [something unintelligible] and it move," I suggest. "Did you see a brown bird today?"

"No, I make brown [something unintelligible] and move it," he says. "Make show."

"Oh! You saw a show? Do you want to write about the show from our field trip Tuesday?"

Vigorous head shake and a frown. "No. I make puppet and make show."

"Aha!! You made a puppet?"

Delighted head nod! It seems that Samuel had been busily working on a craft project during the morning.

"Do you want to show me what you were working on this morning?" I ask him.

Samuel runs over and collects his brown paper bag puppet and then he explains how he made the eyes, mouth, and body.

"How about we write a how-to book about puppets?" I ask. "You could teach everyone how to make one. Let's start with the steps."

BECOMING AN AUTHOR

Samuel and I discuss the steps of his paper bag puppet for more than four minutes before getting paper and pencil. I am thrilled to understand Samuel, and it is clear he is thrilled to be understood. With the ever-increasing demands of the curriculum and the shrinking space for uninterrupted writing time, I could easily let myself think I am wasting those four minutes. But it is important for Samuel to hear his words out loud several times in order to let the sequence, the purpose, and the joy of his book grab hold of him. I believe this joy is key to sustaining our young writers.

Samuel tells me his steps again, and I repeat his phrases as I hold up one finger for each step.

"'You need the bag.' Step one: you need the bag."

"'You make mouth, happy.' Step two: you make mouth, happy."

"'You make eyes, big.' Step three: you make eyes, big."

"'You get square and box and . . .'" Samuel's hands make big gestures. He stands up and ducks his head up and down. I am lost again, uncomprehending.

We spend another two minutes clarifying what Samuel is trying to say. He explains that you need a box for the stage and you duck down behind it and finally make the puppet's mouth move. I make an executive decision and shorten his fourth step. "Step four: you make mouth move."

"All right, Samuel," I say. "That's four steps for making a puppet. Let's say them again." We repeat the steps, this time with Samuel putting up his fingers too.

Eight minutes and we are finally ready for paper and pencil. Samuel knows where the tools for Writing Workshop are kept. He collects the paper, pencil, and stapler and brings them back to me.

We repeat the book title, *How to Make the Puppet Show*, several times. I cowrite with Samuel, helping him remember how to say the words slowly to hear the initial sounds. Then, touching the page for each word, he rereads what he wrote after each word. He is able to independently produce *H to M* (how to make) with the simple prompt, "What do you hear?"

When he gets to the word *the*, I encourage him to use the word wall. I know he understands the word *to*, and *the* is the only other *T* word on our chart. Samuel holds both magnetic words in his hands and looks back and forth a few times before turning to me to say, "This one, *to*. Not this." He copies the word, and we finish his title together. *H to M the PS* (How to Make the Puppet Show). We repeat the process for writing about the first step on the next page, and then I send him on his way to finish the book independently (see Figure 4.3).

As I wander the room to help other writers, I keep an eye on Samuel. He has chosen to sit on the floor at the small round table. I'm not certain he is focused on his story. At one point I force myself to look away from his table because he has called Jeffrey over and the two are playing with Samuel's puppet. I decide to let him remain independent and use what he has accomplished (or did not accomplish) as the mini-lesson for tomorrow.

At the end of Writing Workshop, I call Samuel over and he reads me his work. He has not finished writing the book but he has drawn some of the illustrations and written two pages independently. He is able to retell his entire book verbally. This is an enormous accomplishment for him. I ask him if he would like to share his book with his friends and he eagerly says yes.

Figure 4.3
Samuel independently sounds out the words for his *How to Make the Puppet Show* book.

SPEAKING CONFIDENTLY

After the class gathers in a circle, I ask Samuel to come to the author's chair. I explain to his classmates that at first I did not understand what Samuel's idea was and that we had to talk for a long time. I remind them of the first thing on our class list of the steps in the writing process: "I think about my story." I share how important it was that Samuel made sure I understood what he wanted to say. He repeated himself and found new words to help me comprehend.

Samuel then reads his book to the group.

"How to Make the Puppet Show," he begins. "You need the bag. You need to make mouth and you need eyes."

Samuel has taken the word *you* from the word wall and copied *the* correctly on the additional pages. He had been focused while working independently! He tells us that Jeffrey showed him how to draw the folded part of the mouth and then Samuel explains that he has not yet finished his last page ("You make mouth talk").

He demonstrates the puppet for his peers, and then the puppet and I have a short conversation about our upcoming class field trip. The students love Samuel's story and his performance. Samuel then asks if the class has questions or comments. He thoughtfully chooses four friends to respond. They ask about how he drew the mouth, and Valerie has a suggestion for him: "You need to write, 'Put your hand in it to make it work.'"

Within an hour, Samuel has gone from feeling lost and inept to feeling in control. He has edited and revised his writing. He chose to stay focused on his work, and he asked his classmate for help. He spoke confidently in front of a large group and felt empowered by teaching his friends a skill. He was in command of his ideas, his writing, and his audience. He was an author.

WORTH THE TIME

Taking ten minutes to talk with one writer can be hard to rationalize. I have many other students, all of whom have fabulous books waiting to be discovered. Don't I have to get Sofia to hear the first-letter sounds? Doesn't Adolfo have to stop focusing on his illustrations and starting writing more? And how do I get Jessica to write about something other than flowers and rainbows? I can't spend time "just talking" about writing. Or can I?

Students will develop social and emotional and literacy skills at different rates and at different times. As my students play and work, it is my job to understand their needs and use our interactions to build a solid foundation for introducing the concrete and specific standards of the curriculum. I remind myself that teaching is not "a matter of urgency" but rather a thoughtful and systematic development of an environment that supports learning. An environment that extends beyond today's lesson, beyond this month's science unit, beyond one kindergarten year. An environment where learners of all levels continuously thrive based on authentic communication and meaningful connections.

Chapter 5

GETTING ALONG: BEING PART OF A GROUP

Coming to school for the first time is a wondrous but also scary event for young children. It might involve feelings of excitement, eagerness for independence, and anxiety as well. Sometimes that anxiety can result in reactionary impulses. Suddenly students are part of a twenty-one-member school family, and getting bumped, waiting their turn, and being last can become emotionally charged events. A single day can be an emotional roller coaster of recess highs and spilled-lunch lows; a friendly game of tag can quickly dissolve into bitter shouts of "did!" and "did not!"

I start the year talking and teaching about the social aspect of being part of a group and the emotional concept of empathy. I systematically teach the students about the physical features and sensations that accompany our everyday feelings. It is vital that students learn to recognize how their friends are feeling through body language and facial expressions, because many students do not have the words to express their needs clearly. This helps them dissolve their natural egotistic viewpoints and begin to include others. We then learn to identify our own feelings and watch how our emotions can change in the course of the day. These social and emotional skills lay the foundation for feeling connected and accepted in our classroom. In Figure 5.1, Marcos, Betzy, and Valerie sing one of our favorite lines from the song "Peace Like a River."

Figure 5.1
Marcos, Betzy, and Valerie show they have "love like a mountain" in their souls.

Figure 5.2
Keisy's cheeks are up, her eyes are wide—
we know she's happy!

LEARNING THE VOCABULARY OF EMOTIONS

Empowering students with the vocabulary to clearly share their feelings is a cornerstone of a safe and supporting classroom. We learn how to describe our emotions and use these words in the morning as we greet one another (see Keisy being happy in Figure 5.2): "Your cheeks are up, Valerie. You seem happy this morning." During centers when someone is sharing: "I see Robinson's eyes are big. He likes that you shared the blocks, Marcos." On the playground as the rules of tag gets confusing: "I can't see Nikki's face because her head is down. I bet she's sad."

Some children struggle with the language of emotions much more than others. Josue often barged into the classroom, announcing his arrival in a loud voice, "I'm here and the bus was late!" or "Did everyone see my new backpack? James, look! My new backpack" as he shoved the Mario Kart backpack into James's face. Josue's voice was always too loud, his actions too large, and his attempts to make friends too forced. He was immature and egotistic in the give-and-take of friendship. Josue's "stage of friendship" (Gurian and Formanek 1983) was firmly based in the three- and four-year-old range. He viewed friendship solely in the present moment: "James is my friend because we are doing stamps now." Josue's five- and six-year-old classmates, on the other hand, already had an understanding of friendship being based on shared interests and lasting over time.

Our lessons on discovering and learning about the similarities we all share did not seem to reach Josue. He would sit quietly during share time but it was clear he was not listening, not present to the person speaking. He didn't seem to care. I realized I couldn't force him to care; he would mature in his own time; But maybe I could create baby steps to see if we were making progress.

When Josue was the class helper or the line leader for the day, I would allow him to choose a buddy to help him. I had a small cup with the children's names written on Popsicle sticks, and I would let Josue choose from three sticks. This way Josue was not overwhelmed with choices and I could ensure that everyone had a chance to be his buddy. Throughout the day, I would find extra things for Josue to do (return books to the library, clean the paintbrushes, tidy up the nonfiction books). I would point out how well the buddies were doing. "It's great to see you giving books to Sofia to carry, Josue. I bet that feels good, doesn't it, Sofia?"

In the following days, at Writing Workshop, I would suggest that (read: entice, persuade, make) Josue write about one of the jobs he did with his buddy. We would discuss, write, and illustrate the "very best part" and then publish it (read: make a photocopy). Josue would give his story to his buddy to put in his or her book box or take home. Over time these strategies helped him get a better grip on his emotions.

ANALYZING STUDENTS' EMOTIONS AND CLASSROOM INTERVENTIONS

Figure 5.3 shows a graphic representation of the reflective process that I go through as I consider the possible causes of students' misbehaviors, observe their interpersonal relationships, and think of actions I could take to address their social and emotional needs and redirect their behavior. In the following section, I explore different sets of teacher reflections related to the Friendship Workshop topic of Getting Along: Being Part of a Group and discuss examples of how students' interactions might play out in the classroom.

Behaviors

Parallel play (plays next to, not with, other students)

Forcing way into groups

Being "busy" (avoiding contact)

Disconnected from group

Figure 5.3
Being Part
of a Group

Reflection Questions

When does it occur?   With whom?

What exactly is the student doing?

Is student aware of own actions?

Aware of others' feelings?

Aware of others' needs?

Possible Needs

Need to feel significant   Calming sensations

Social vocabulary   Attention stamina

Understanding of community

STAYING FOCUSED

Reflection Questions

Does the student have the ability to stay focused on preferred tasks, or is he always distracted? Does he lose attention in all group sizes or when the group is large? Is the beginning or end of the day harder for him? These broad questions help me look at the general issue and not the specific behavior yet.

Possible Needs

Some children have an overdeveloped sense of importance and can demand attention from everyone all the time. Other children are the opposite: they don't feel connected or important, and they remain silent and in the background. Helping these students build connections will not only enhance their social skills but also improve their academic engagement as well.

Possible Actions

When we look past the larger obvious connections (a friend who also has a big brother or comes from the same country) and point out the smaller things that link them to their classmates, we reinforce the uniqueness of each child. For example, I might point out that his method for solving the math problem was the same as Julio's or that her backpack is the same as Abigail's. Sometimes these small connections are more relative to young children and help them feel safe to assert themselves more.

STUDENT ENGAGEMENT

Reflection Questions

Do my lessons drag on and on with too many instructions so that I start sounding like Charlie Brown's teacher: "Wa, waa, waaa, waa"? Have they learned a pattern from my behavior? Do I only call on the front of the group? Or just the students who have quick answers? Have I fallen into accepting her as just a quiet child because I have to deal with three "energetic" answerers?

Possible Needs

Young students' attention spans are elastic and will vary throughout the day. I try to make sure when giving directions or having book discussions that the time frames are developmentally appropriate for the grade level. I try to think of my own behavior in a boring meeting, as my mind suddenly starts considering how fascinating it is that the eraser is attached to my pencil!

Possible Actions

When we provide short, precise directions and interactive instructions, we help students build stamina, because the brain does not have time to be distracted. We can also break projects into sections with a short, whole-group gathering in between the sections.

FIDGETING

Reflection Questions

Does the student act out when she is disconnected (poking neighbors, tossing pencils into the air), or does she turn inward (hyperfocus on shoelaces, stare aimlessly)? What is she doing, specifically? I might keep track of exactly what she is doing for a week. Does she always play with something in her hands?

Does she squirm on her knees and feet while looking out the window? Does she recite the name poster when she is supposed to be looking at the math problem on the Smart Board?

Possible Needs

Some students need to move to think. Eric Jensen, in *Teaching with the Brain in Mind*, explains that physical movement and cognitive learning have similar characteristics within the brain. The cerebellum is the part of the brain most associated with physical movement. To perform a jump or dive requires the mental processes of predicting, ordering, timing, and practicing, to name a few. These tasks use similar neurons and take similar pathways when memorizing the names of the U.S. presidents or learning to add three-digit numbers. "Amazingly, the part of the brain that processes movement is the same part of the brain that processes learning" (Jensen 2005, 61).

Possible Actions

It's important to bring positive attention to the change in behavior rather than focus negative attention on the child. Being discreet and polite can go a long way toward shifting a fidgety student's behavior. Placing a hand on the student's shoulder while giving directions or regularly walking close to the table can refocus a wandering mind. A code word or action discussed in private can make the reminders feel less like punishment. Bryan and I set up a signal that reminded me of playing tag with a toddler. It was the familiar two fingers pointing at my eyes, then flipping to point at his eyes. We created the phrase "I'm going to catch you . . . doing it right!"

Some teachers have found that a thick rubber band worn on a student's wrist during meetings can provide controlled stimulation for some students. In my experience, this is too distracting for younger students, but upper elementary children can find it helpful. Of course, specific rules need to be put in place about how the tool will be used. For example, it must always stay on the wrist, must never be given to a friend, must always be quiet, and so on.

UNDERSTANDING GROUP DYNAMICS

Reflection Questions

Can the student tell you what he was doing (fidgeting or staring)? When you refocus the student, can he acknowledge that he was not paying attention? Some students might not understand that being part of a group is something that we practice all the time, not just at Morning Meeting or during read-alouds. Checking in before the mini-lesson with a quick comment, "Josue, I'm going to ask you about the recording sheet so be listening," is one way to draw in Josue and establish accountability. Checking in after a discussion with an open-ended question, "Josue, what part of Jocelyn's experiment did you like?" sets up Josue for success (ideally!). Drawing attention to the moments when the student is connected and naming the action can also help connect him to the group and the lessons.

Possible Needs

Students want to know they are important. Sometimes certain people or activities can make children feel unimportant and they will shut down. Some students may "zone out," some may remove themselves from the group, and some may try to be part of every group. These behaviors may indicate a lack of connection to the group as well as a lack of connection to the learning. If we provide time and support for students to connect their home life to their school family, we can help them through difficult or exciting social developments.

Possible Actions

When I taught multiage K–1 with Christy Hermann Thompson, we shared students for different parts of the day. Daniel (not his real name) was "officially" Christy's student but his behavior affected both communities. He was a student as yet unidentified with autism, and Christy and I struggled to help him feel connected to others. Daniel had difficulty with peer connections; he could be excessively stubborn when using materials, he could be verbally loud and disruptive, and he often put things in his mouth that were inappropriate and made his peers (and us) cringe. His classmates often found it unbearable to work with him and many lessons were interrupted or ruined.

Christy and I spent many afternoons nibbling on Goldfish crackers and drinking tea, trying to figure out how to help Daniel feel more connected. We tried a buddy system, a personal checklist of behaviors, and a reward system for working in a group, but nothing stuck, nothing produced a lasting result. Somehow, in our ache of failing Daniel, we hit upon the idea of helping the other students help Daniel.

I remembered when a colleague, Melissa Fleischer, had a particularly difficult child in her class of fourth graders. One day she held a class meeting, without the student, and allowed the children to be candid in their feelings. They were honest and civil in their descriptions of the damage this student had caused. With the situation out in the open, Melissa and her students were able to form a bond of trust that helped them handle that difficult year.

Christy and I decided to try the same thing. We had a meeting without Daniel to ask the class how they felt when working with him. They were honest and respectful, sharing their frustration and annoyance when he didn't listen, demanded his way, or wouldn't pay attention. After a long round of discussing what wasn't working, we prompted them to identify when Daniel was helpful (he loved to illustrate things), when he played well (he was good at tag), and some of Daniel's strengths (his Lego constructions were magnificent).

We discussed what his "bad days" looked like and made connections to our own "bad days." I remember Yohana, who was the third eldest of six siblings, saying, "There are just some days I wish I didn't have to share with everyone!" We used these connections to strengthen the students' empathy and acceptance for someone who was different from them. We decided instead of our assigning Daniel to a group, Christy and I would ask who would like to be in Daniel's group. We hoped to accomplish two things: (1) a student who was not feeling particularly patient that day could say "No, thank you," and (2) Daniel would sense at least some of his peers wanting to be with him.

Did it all go fabulously? No. After all, the children were only five and six years old. They had selfish desires and limitations of their own to navigate. But it did cushion some of the most trying days. The strategy also taught Christy and me the importance of truly including the students in making a community. My dog-eared and highlighted copy of Ralph Petersen's *Life in a Crowded Place*, puts it like this, "The process is circular: as the group comes together, the individual is strengthened, and as individuals grow in confidence and expression, they increase their caring contributions to the group" (Petersen 1992, 66).

Chapter 6

EMPATHY

A treasured book in my professional library is *Nonviolent Communication: A Language of Compassion* by Marshall Rosenberg (2003), the founder of the Center for Nonviolent Communication. Rosenberg studied the causes of violence and ways to reduce it. Through his research, he came to understand that language contributes to an atmosphere of aggression. For example, when we use language that "blames, shames, criticizes, and demands" (Hart and Kindle Hodson 2004, 6), we are often reacting to an internal emotional discomfort that blocks our natural compassion and stops our connection to others. Learning empathy shifts our language to be more honest, forgiving, and respectful.

The first "official" empathy lessons in our Friendship Workshop start with an in-depth look at facial expressions and body language. There are social skills programs available in print and on the Internet that have format photographs for just this purpose (I used photos from the Second Step program [Committee for Children 2014], available at www.cfchildren.org/second-step/aspx). The photographs are large (18 by 20 inches), close-up images of children's faces in various emotional states. We spend the lesson observing a photograph of a specific emotional facial expression—sadness, for example. We focus on describing the physical aspects we observe. We use small mirrors to mimic the emotion on our own face and then watch and describe our partners' faces as they express the same emotion. I describe situations that would induce the emotion and watch the physical changes our faces and bodies make. We continue this process each week, covering seven basic emotions of *happy, sad, mad, excited, disgusted*, *surprised*, and *afraid*, and I make certain we stay focused on the physical features, not our perceptions about why someone might feel this way.

One year, after we had studied all the emotions, each student chose an emotion to illustrate with paper masks. We took photographs of the students holding up their completed masks, and then the students wrote statements to go along with their emotions (see Figures 6.1 and 6.2). For example, "I feel angry when my baby brother breaks my crayons" or "I feel happy when my mom takes me to McDonald's." These activities strengthened lessons about how our feelings are universal. We later shared the book with several other classes (see Figure 6.3).

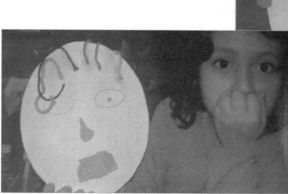

Figure 6.1
Mutaz has a furrowed brow and his lips are tight together to show his mad face.

Figure 6.2
Rawala's mask has big eyes and an open mouth to show she's scared.

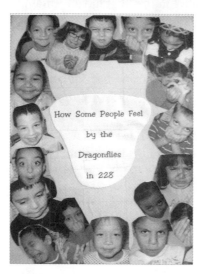

Figure 6.3
The students wrote a book, *How Some People Feel*, after our Friendship Workshop lessons on empathy.

LEARNING TO FORGIVE

Thich Nhat Hahn, a Vietnamese monk and peace activist, writes, "When another person makes you suffer, it is because he suffers deeply within himself, and his suffering is spilling over. He does not need punishment; he needs help. That's the message he is sending" (Thich Nhat Hanh 1998, 196). *The Recess Queen* by Alexis O'Neill and illustrated by Laura Huliska-Beith is a fabulous book to teach this concept. The bold illustrations and rhythmic lines grab students from the start and lead to discussions about what it feels like to be left out and why someone who is mean may feel sad and lonely too.

This does not mean that we have to accept inappropriate or hurtful behaviors. Rather, we address each incident separately from any other incident and forgive the offender. His Holiness the Dalai Lama writes, "Look at children. Of course they may quarrel, but generally speaking they do not harbor ill feelings as much or as long as adults do. Most adults have the advantage of education over children, but what is the use of an education if they show a big smile while hiding negative feelings deep inside? Children don't usually act in such a manner. If they feel angry with someone, they express it, and then it is finished. They can still play with that person the following day" (Nuckols 2010, 161).

As teachers, we want to show students how to express their anger in appropriate ways that lead to healthy resolutions. Most mistakes in elementary school are minor, but even cruel bullying can be handled with compassion. I remember the class bully who tormented my son, Griffin, and other children in his third-grade class. The school and the teachers were doing what they could to address the situation and eventually they were able to find a more appropriate school for the bully to attend.

Until that time, it broke my heart to see my son come home scared, insecure, and defeated every day. I tried to give him some tools to get through his distress. We talked and meditated and drew and talked. In the end what helped my son was the statement "Someone who feels good about themselves would not act like this. His heart is hurting." This did not mean Griffin had to like the boy. He did not have to play with him or work with him or even forgive him. He could separate himself from the bully's actions. Griffin learned how to protect himself when he chose to feel compassion instead of adopting the same angry and mean emotions as the bully.

In our classrooms we must be willing to bring these strong emotions to the surface of our school community. People judge and form attitudes quickly; it is our nature. By discussing powerful emotions early in the school year, *before* those attitudes are established, we can build the foundation of our community with empathy and acceptance in place of judgment and rejection.

EMPATHY CHART

Figure 6.4 shows a graphic representation of the reflective process that I go through as I consider the possible causes of students' misbehaviors, observe their interpersonal relationships, and think of actions I could take to address their social and emotional needs in terms of empathy and then to redirect their behavior. In the following section, I explore different sets of teacher reflections related to the Friendship Workshop topic of empathy and discuss examples of how students' interactions might play out in the classroom.

SELFISHNESS

Reflection Questions

Lack of empathy can seem like selfishness or bossiness or manipulation. As young students grow and mature (sometime not as fast as we'd like!), they put their hypotheses of how they fit into the world to the test on a regular basis. Developmental thoughts such as the following might be behind some typical selfish behaviors we see in the classroom:

Brené Brown on Empathy

Behaviors

Selfishness

Using uncaring words

Showing off

Teasing others

Figure 6.4
Developing
Empathy

Reflection Questions

When does it occur?   With whom?

What exactly is the student doing?

Is the student aware of his/her own actions?

Jealous of a specific student?   Fear there's not enough?

Is the student aware that his/her
behaviors hurt others?

Possible Needs

Time to adjust to school culture

Establish personal space

Lessen egotistical view   Sense of belonging

Understand responsibilities of the
classroom community

- "If I don't hide the last puzzle piece, then how will I get rewarded for being the one who finished it?"

- "If I grab all the markers, then people have to ask me for one and that gives me power."

- "When I only share with Nikki, then she will be my friend and no one else's *ever*."

Possible Needs

I often try to form a statement from the child's perspective. I ask myself, What would make her happy right now? or What is it he *really* wants? These questions can help flush out what might be hidden beneath the misbehaviors.

As teachers, we need to see if there is a pattern in students' selfishness. Does the behavior occur during the morning before they have had time to adjust to being with twenty-two other people? Does it happen when they are with specific children? Do they cling to materials during special instructional periods (music, art, and so on), or does the possessiveness just affect classroom materials?

Possible Actions

Mornings can often be chaotic and rushed and can leave us with a subtle sense of agitation. I know leaving just seven minutes late in the morning made my commute in Northern Virginia a nightmare. My shoulders would hitch up and my jaw would tighten as the tick, tick, tick of my mental clock reminded me that I was never going to be able to set up my lessons in time. Listening to Jasmine ramble on about her new baby sister was not enjoyable on those mornings.

Now, imagine you are six years old and sleepy and being barraged with orders and questions upon flopping out of bed: get dressed, hurry up and eat, where is your backpack, what do you mean you can only find one shoe? You get on the bus where it is loud and bumpy and smelly, then shuffled into a room about the size of a living room and told to immediately interact nicely with the other twenty people there . . . Sheesh, I'd be a little cranky too!

My colleague Christy Hermann Thompson started the mornings for her first graders with a transition time. She read somewhere that a teacher called this session "Breathing In," and it allowed the children to ease into the school day. Christy would set up special stations for the children to choose from. One time it was a veterinarian clinic with stuffed animals, another time a post office with stamps and packages of different sizes. The science table and library were always available. The children were free to choose to work or talk or just sit. Christy remembers one morning in particular when Jose, usually happy and boisterous, sat in the bean bag chair, not moving. When Christy checked in with him, Jose revealed that he had spent a difficult night at home. Christy scheduled time for Jose to speak with the counselor that morning. "By giving them time and choices, I could observe and see what mood they were in," Christy told me. This method enabled her to connect to Jose and adjust his day to respect his sensitive mood.

Allowing a morning work period gives students time to adjust from their home lives to the rules and expectations of school life. We can provide an open choice time or a worksheet reinforcing yesterday's lessons. We can require it be finished before Morning Meeting, or let the children finish it for homework. I have found it best to make the activity an independent lesson that balances casual conversation with some light structure. I use connect-the-dot, color-by-numbers, or cut-and-glue matching pages. These simple activities give the children a "soft period" of learning while allowing me to touch base and get a feel for their emotional states.

For example, it is annoying and frustrating for me when students do not share, because clearly a box of sixty-four crayons means there are enough shades of blue for everyone to get one. But for children who don't yet know how to think beyond their own needs, this reaction does not feel true. If the basic lessons on sharing and waiting for a turn are not helping a particular student, I explicitly set aside a double set of the materials so that she can have her own materials while learning to trust that she will get what she needs. This is much like the "teach from the known" concept in Reading Recovery training.

If a child is distraught about needing all the red counting bears and I force her into sharing, not only will she not learn how to share, but she won't retain the math lesson either. The "known" in this case is that there will always be enough for me to do my work. The trust will come from hearing statements from me such as "Maritza, can I borrow five red bears to tell my story, please? I will give them back when I am finished." And afterward, "Thank you for sharing your bears. I know you like them but you helped me teach everyone the math lesson today. You were so helpful when you shared."

Teachers have hundreds of ways of storing classroom materials. Some use group bins for crayons and glue sticks; others have individual boxes for each student. Most of us set up what feels logical to us, and the students adjust. Except for Katy. Katy was so possessive of classroom materials that I would find all the purple crayons stuffed inside the battery compartment of the listening center player! She was quite crafty—and annoying!

I like to keep tables clean and empty, so our shared writing and coloring materials were stored in a bookcase located in the middle of the room. Because Katy needed to have her own tools close at hand, I bought a simple plastic pencil box at a dollar store, and Katy decorated it with stickers and markers. She kept all her writing tools in the box and left it on her favorite table in the room. No one else needed the materials or asked for them, but if I had had more than a few students who struggled with possessiveness, I hope I would have adjusted my own preferences for what would benefit the class as a whole.

A small way to reduce the anxiety some students have about getting materials is to always be sure you have more than you need. If we are making covers for our stories out of colored construction paper I bring twenty-four pieces to the carpet even though I only have twenty-one students. Such small gestures send a clear message of respect: the last student doesn't "get stuck" with a green cover when he really wanted blue.

POSSESSIVENESS

Reflection Questions

Establishing territory includes racing to be first in line, grabbing the first worksheet, claiming the rocking chair every day during Reading Workshop. Do the students *need* to be first in line? Do they feel "safer" in that spot? Feel a sense of power? Do they behave better when they are first in line? Do they jeer at others for being last?

Possible Needs

Establishing territory is deeply connected to wanting to feel significant. Students often believe that "If I am first in line, then the teacher *sees* me." I often have casual playful conversations with the line leader as we walk to art class or lunch. Wanting or needing attention can be a driving force for some students' misconduct. Some race to the rocking chair every day because they sense that "If I have the chair, then you want to BE me." The power in having the coveted classroom possession can be intoxicating. Shifting students out of this egotistical stage of development can be fun.

Possible Actions

I might try overly enthusiastic statements such as "Yohanna, you are awesome! You let Nhi have the rocking chair today [as Yohanna stares daggers at Nhi in the chair because I am still holding Yohanna's hand!]. You are so kind to share that favorite chair with a friend!" followed by a giant bear hug. Or "Amner! You the man! Waiting there like a frozen statue so everyone else can get their folder first" (as his hands are hovering over the writing bin in a pouncing position). Constant casual comments such as these can reinforce the lesson that thinking about others and being part of a group are enjoyable and rewarding experiences.

CONSISTENT RULES AND PROCEDURES

Reflection Questions

I ask myself if my classroom layout includes quiet individual spots as well as small clusters of work areas. Have I established clear procedures in our room (how we will distribute and collect materials, specific jobs for students, and so on)?

Possible Needs

Students need predictability. This desire is greater than just knowing the day's schedule or knowing when the upcoming field trip will happen. They need to know very specifically how to do what we as teachers often think are very obvious procedures: how to hang up a backpack and coat so they stay on the hook, how to put the caps on markers so they don't dry out, how to put writing folders away so papers don't spill out when they are picked up.

Responsive Classroom offers a fabulous approach for creating classrooms that are organized, predictable, and consistent, which allows students to feel confident and safe. In *The First Six Weeks of School*, Paula Denton and Roxann Kriete explain, "[W]e want children, from the first day of school, to feel secure and successful because they know the rules of the culture" (2000, 30). Modeling is a very specific technique for establishing fixed classroom behaviors, such as pushing chairs in, handling library books, getting drinks after P.E., and so on. I have suffered the consequences of rushing through teaching that last procedure, and for months I had to stand guard at the water fountain like a Secret Service agent!

If a certain procedure is not working smoothly (or is completely out of hand), then stop and reteach it. Admit to the students, "The writing folders get knocked over every day. I apologize for not showing you exactly what I wanted to happen at the end of Writing Workshop. Watch me." Model the precise behavior, using detailed actions and language. Ask the children what they noticed and allow them to model the behavior while their peers watch. Again, ask what they noticed and discuss how the new ("and improved") behavior will help the community. I had to push myself past the feeling that I was wasting time and remember that even Paula Denton, author of three Responsive Classroom books, had a year when "It was the first six weeks all year long" (Denton and Kriete 2000, 6). I took a few days to reteach the behaviors by starting and ending Writing Workshop with modeling, discussing, and reflecting on how we had behaved. Although it made the actual writing time shorter on those days, we ended up with longer work blocks, smoother transitions, and less adult interference in the months that followed.

HURTFUL WORDS AND TEASING

Reflection Questions

Asking the students to try to verbalize why they are so possessive can sometimes reveal new understandings. What will help the students feel successful at this activity? Do they feel stressed when they have to wait for help or materials? Does finishing first make them feel "smarter"? Do they associate not knowing with being "dumb"?

Possible Needs

Many times students' lack of empathy stems from leftover "hurts." They were picked last for tag at recess so they now tease the person last in line. They didn't get to sit next to someone at lunch so they leave no room for him at the science table.

"You're not my friend." We've all heard that phrase uttered in our classrooms. It's the default expression when young students are hurt and angry. If we want to reinforce empathy, we must stop what we are doing and address the situation. The statement is not only hurtful but also untrue. The children are friends. However, when hurt they may lack the words to express themselves effectively so they lash out.

Possible Actions

Give each child a chance to explain the situation and then clarify the specific problem. Teach students to be specific and say, for example, "I don't like that you left me out at recess" to help them feel in control of the situation while staying connected to the other person.

I remember one student, Gavin, who was fast to react, often in the form of snide remarks. He could be sweet, but he was usually short-tempered, ill-prepared for sharing, and overly energetic (Tasmanian devil energy). Sticker charts, separate seating, buddy systems—you name it, I tried it. But Gavin was smart and he learned quickly how to work the system, so the incentives fell away and his modus operandi of teasing and making rude comments would return.

One day during Friendship Workshop when Rabia was chosen to hold the chart, Gavin said loudly, "I can't see the words because of her fat fingers!" I knew he was hurt that he wasn't chosen to be the helper, but there was no excuse for that behavior. I looked at him and said, "Gavin, did you just hit Rabia?"

Gavin was appalled, "No, I didn't hit her!"

"Then what did you do?" I asked.

"I didn't *do* anything" (the sarcastic remarks were so annoying).

"I think you hit her. If you didn't hit her, what did you do?" After several rounds of this, he finally admitted what he had said.

"Oh," I said, nodding my head slowly, "your angry words, they are just like hitting someone. You hit her heart with those hurtful words."

My comments didn't really make an impression on Gavin, but they did affect the other children. They started using the phrase with one another when someone teased them: "Those words hurt my heart. Please stop." (See Figure 6.5 for the simple phrase that Jen Tustin Parks's class came up with to tell a friend to stop.)

BECOMING INCLUSIVE WITHIN GROUPS

Reflection Questions

Young children who have underdeveloped empathy skills may be unaccustomed to being in a large group. Have the students been in a school setting before? Do they come from families where they receive a lot of undivided attention? Are they aware of others around them, or do they operate within their own sphere?

Figure 6.5
Jen Tustin Parks's fun and friendly poster helps students ask for personal space.

Possible Needs

Students who struggle with sharing have not yet learned that others have different goals and desires than they do.

Possible Actions

Sometimes the only action to take is to be empathetic myself. I slow down and take the time to appreciate all the changes, expectations, and worries my students face on a daily basis. I check in with myself to see if my expectations are too high or too many or too fast. I reflect on how I felt during the day to see if I was unconsciously creating a stressful atmosphere.

Although it may seem heavy-handed when most of the class does understand how to share and think of others, we must remember that these social and emotional skills are skills to be learned. Just like teaching fractions or how to make predictions, we must scaffold our students' learning with direct instruction, differentiation, and an abundance of laughter and patience.

LITERACY CONNECTIONS: BEING PART OF A GROUP AND EMPATHY CONNECT TO ORAL STORYTELLING AND PRESENTING A PERFORMANCE

To support these new understandings of empathetic connections and being part of a group, the first literacy activity we do together is to listen to and tell stories. Our oral language practice includes repetition of phrases from books, songs, and poems in order to create a safe place to speak. Reading Workshop consists mostly of whole-group read-alouds as we discuss the setting, the characters, and the emotions in various texts. We retell and spontaneously act out stories at choice time, at recess, and during Math Workshop. The class then chooses a favorite book to present a simple original production to share with other classes. Using a mentor text, such as *Owl Babies* by Martin Waddell, *Where the Wild Things Are* by Maurice Sendak, or other classic texts with a simple story line and a repetitious phrase, we create playful ways to help children develop the skills needed to read and write. We read and reread our book many times to help learn how to retell a story in sequence. The students build comprehension skills as we navigate the most important parts of the story. I introduce letter-sound correspondences as we use community writing to write the title and speech bubbles for our play. Sharing, cooperating on the same project, taking care of materials, and other skills needed to be part of a group are at the forefront of these Reading Workshops. I must trust my gut that the literacy skills will develop over time and that establishing empathy now will ensure smooth workshops later.

We paint a background setting for the play and create paper puppets or masks for the characters. (Figure 6.6 shows how Kathy Birge's students made masks for the performance of "The Noisy Monkey.") We choose simple actions for the characters and reenact them as a whole group so there is no "star" role. This method provides a safe setting for everyone to participate at their own comfort level as we travel from class to class performing our play. (The plays last between five and eight minutes, and that includes question and answer time!) It is the first opportunity as a new "school family" to share and delight in the joy of literature together.

Writing Workshop continues our focus on being part of a group and practicing empathy by telling personal stories. I do most of the talking during these first weeks to help establish the purpose and format of the workshop. It is important in the beginning weeks of each school year that the students learn *what* a story is—a message-making tool to share ourselves with one another. When I share a story about losing my car in a big parking lot the children hear the worry in my voice and see the nervousness in my motions, and they feel connected to those sensations. Through my storytelling the students learn about *me* as a

Figure 6.6
Kathy Birge's class presents "The Noisy Monkey" for students and teachers.

person. I tell funny stories, sad stories, and stories about my family that shows the students I am just like them. I have birthdays, I make mistakes, I fall down, I get surprised, I even cry.

The children watch and listen as I tell and retell and retell my story, adding words because of their questions, changing my beginning to help them understand the ending, using motions to show the fullness of the moment. This storytelling unit develops a healthy and successfully managed classroom because it is through sharing my stories that the children learn to trust. Through carefully chosen stories they take notice again and again that I am not expecting perfection, I do not have all the answers, and I am not afraid to share my mistakes. This is the beginning of knowing that they can share their emotions and make mistakes too.

Storytelling incorporates everything we will be doing as writers throughout the year: planning, revising, editing, illustrating, and publishing. I am teaching them how complete sentences sound, how certain words or phrases are so fun to repeat, how a story is thrilling and makes us question, wonder, and laugh together. Again, I need to trust that literacy is a cumulative development and that learning is more effective when it is free from stress and anxiety. We will learn to sound out words, use the word wall, capitalize proper nouns, and use punctuation, but for now I want to let the children know that writing, like reading, is a "message-getting problem-solving activity which increases in power and flexibility the more it is practiced" (Clay 1991, 6) and it is fun.

Storytelling allows us to connect to similar life events, problems, and joys. These connections build a community that respects and supports one another. I believe it is my responsibility to show my students not just *how*, but *why* their stories are powerful and need to be heard. The more authentic their learning, the more they will want to express themselves and be understood. The more connected they are to our classroom community, the more they will care about what we do there.

"Storytelling is clearly a social experience with oral narrative, incorporating linguistic features that display a 'sophistication that goes beyond the level of conversation.' And for this reason storytelling acts as an effective building block easing the journey from oracy to literacy" (Phillips n.d.).

"Easing the journey from oracy to literacy"—what a wonderful phrase!

Chapter 7

KINDNESS

Being kind is about having a strong heart. It shows the world the way we feel about ourselves and each other. Being kind also has a ripple effect—it spreads beyond ourselves—and it has a rubber-band effect—kindness comes back to us when we display it first.

Most times, when something happens by accident at school, the victims just want an acknowledgment. They're not really hurt or even bothered by the event; they just don't want to be jostled and ignored. When teaching kindness, I most often use direct episodes from the classroom or cafeteria, or the mother lode—the playground. For most conflicts, the students already know what happened and who was involved. Using pretend "Dick and Jane" characters negates the importance of the lessons I want to share with my students, so I have learned to be real.

As a side note, I have had a recurring conversation over the years with colleagues about "calling a kid out on the carpet." Some teachers believe it is rude or belittling to publicly discuss a student's misbehavior. Although I agree that there are certainly times when discreet discussions are more appropriate, I usually feel confident in addressing a situation with the whole class because of the foundation of empathy and compassion we have already established. For example, Mario knew after he pushed Adam and caused him to get a skinned knee that I was going to hold him accountable for his actions during our class meeting that afternoon. He trusted that I respected him and wanted to help him *and* that I was going to make him listen to how his behavior affected all his friends, not just Adam. My intent was not to punish or belittle Mario; quite the opposite. I wanted to help Mario hear and feel in an honest and supportive environment that he plays too rough and his friends don't like it. Identifying, acknowledging, and reenacting the actual misdeed allows all students to be involved in the problem-solving aspect of classroom behavior.

SELF-TALK

The first person we must be kind to is ourselves. When students grumble, using phrases such as "I can't do this" or "I'm always the last one," they have fixated on a perceived shortcoming and are at risk of thinking of the behavior as a permanent state of being. It's true that they may not be able to complete the task or be the first one to finish their work at the time, but shifting their self-talk to reflect the impermanence of the situation is powerful. I rephrase a child's talk whenever I can. "I can't" becomes "I'm trying" and "I'm always last" becomes "I want to be faster." It's a small but necessary shift that can help students be gentler with themselves.

Self-talk is already part of our academic dialogue, so bringing it into Friendship Workshop merely reinforces how it helps us learn. I explain that self-portraits represent how we see ourselves and self-talk how we feel about ourselves. I show a photo of a situation (many of the large-scale photos in social and emotional learning programs can be used for this purpose). Perhaps a student is distracted by two loud students or two students are pulling the same book from the library shelf. We discuss what is happening and what students might say to themselves to help fix the situation. The children usually suggest the "right" answers: "She can ask them to be quiet" or "They can share the book." This shows me that they know what to do but need help remembering to act appropriately.

Self-talk is about turning the "right" answers into the "right" actions. We brainstorm words to use in our heads when we find ourselves in frustrating situations. We also name the feeling and a solution.

Some phrases we have created include these:

I feel _____ (angry / happy / hurt) right now. I do / do not like this feeling.
I want to _____ (give up / sing / scream).
I can _____ (tell a friend / run a mile / try later).

Afterward, we draw a picture of a time when we used self-talk (or could have), and I type up a thought bubble filled with the students' self-talk words. The students take this graphic home and share with their families how self-talk helps them.

"EXCUSE ME, CAN I HELP?"

Being kind also means being polite. "Excuse me" is easy to say and communicates a lot of empathy, but children are often unaware of these words and how they can help resolve conflicts. I sprinkle small lessons throughout the day as I see opportunities to practice being kind. Transitions such as lining up for recess or going home offer examples every day. Unless I run my classroom like my son's boot camp drill instructor, there will be bumping and crowding and complaining when it's time to get our backpacks to go home. So when I see Marcos lean directly across Betzy's face to grab his backpack I seize the moment.

"Marcos, come back here," I say. I make him retrace ten steps to the edge of the carpet. "Betzy was in front of your backpack and you shoved right past her. That's not kind. This time when you go to get your backpack, what can you say to Betzy if she is in your way?"

"I dunno," Marco answers as he stares at the carpet with great boredom.

"Would this work? 'Yo, Betzy! Move it!'"

Marcos and the group of students around us laugh heartily and assure me that would *not* work. "What about, 'Excuse me, Betzy'?" Marcos grins slightly and nods his assent. "Okay, so when you go to your backpack I'm going to be listening and I want to hear if it works, deal?"

I watch as Marcos walks over to Betzy, looks back at me (I put one hand up to my ear and scrunch up my eyes to let him know I'm listening hard) and he mumbles, "Excuse me, Betzy." Betzy, who has been oblivious to this conversation because she has Hello Kitty makeup in her bag (that lesson will wait for another day), turns and says, "Oh, sorry, Marcos." I let out a whoop and double thumbs-up to Marcos, who rolls his eyes and shakes his head at his goofy teacher, but I can tell you, after a few of those lessons, he stopped shoving in front of people (at least when I was looking—ha!). Again, practicing in a lighthearted manner when emotions are low can increase the chances that students will remember the easy feeling of being kind. (Figure 7.1 shows Marcos helping Betzy with her backpack.)

PLANNING AHEAD

One time I had—or, so I thought—a brilliant idea. One of our kindness rules was that even if you didn't work in a certain area you could still help and clean it up. Several students were ending up in arguments during cleanup time because they wanted to tidy their materials by themselves, but people were grabbing things to try to help them. I thought an "authentic" re-creation would help solve things.

I put a box filled with books in the middle of the floor and asked Emma to move it to a nearby table. It was too heavy and too large for her and she clearly needed help. The children quickly dashed to her side, shouting, "I can help!" and "I can do it," and the flurry of activity was amusing to watch as they fumbled about. I stopped the commotion and asked what they noticed.

Figure 7.1
Marcos returns Betzy's backpack after knocking it to the ground.

Giselle said, "The box was heavy. Emma needed help." Ben added, "She couldn't do it alone. It was too big." We discussed how it feels good inside when you help someone, and Emma shared that getting help felt good for her too.

I then placed an empty box in the middle of the floor and asked Anthony to move it (I had secretly asked three friends to jump in and help him). As Anthony lifted the box, the three classmates grabbed the box to "help," and Anthony got annoyed. "I can do it! Leave it!" and before it dissolved into fisticuffs I intervened and asked what happened. Several versions of the situation were shouted out at once, and I had to use my "outdoor voice" to bring things back under control.

We finally got around to discussing how helping someone who doesn't need it may not feel good, but the lesson was less than stellar. For days, what Anthony remembered was that his friends grabbed things from him when he didn't need help.

In hindsight, it was silly of me to introduce a surprise lesson with my students. I should have explained to the class—and to Anthony—what was going to happen. Instead of waiting for spontaneous reactions (or spontaneous combustion, as it turned out), I could have asked some students to act out the frustration and then I could have made the point about asking to help. Or, I could have been the one to model becoming frustrated when someone helped without asking.

I never tried that lesson again as a formal Friendship Workshop lesson, but in subsequent years I used the same language when an incident happened in the classroom naturally. I would stop the student who was grabbing the Legos to help clean up and explain to the small group that sometimes helping isn't helping unless you ask first. After several weeks of small-group, real-life lessons, I brought the idea into Friendship Workshop and we came up with the simple rule of asking, "Can I help?" before touching someone else's work. It became an easy flowing phrase whenever it was time to put materials away, hand out snacks, or participate in other organizational activities.

CREATING SPACE FOR FORGIVENESS

Teaching students (okay, *drilling* students) to simply say, "I'm sorry. It was an accident. Are you okay?" does not solve all confrontations in the classroom, but the expression builds on our foundation of empathy and creates a space for forgiveness. Self-talk is the first step to shifting external teacher guidance to a more self-reliant method of making good choices. Our work to describe feelings has prepared students for self-talk; they now know how to pause for a moment before reacting. The phrases we use are similar to our problem-solving dialogues ("I feel_____." "I would like _____."). Self-talk helps students be honest and kind when facing their own mistakes, which then makes it easier to accept the mistakes of others.

Figure 7.2 shows a graphic representation of the reflective process that I go through as I consider the possible causes of students' misbehaviors, observe their interpersonal relationships, and think of actions I could take to address their social and emotional needs in terms of kindness and then to redirect their behavior. In the following section, I explore different sets of teacher reflections related to the Friendship Workshop topic of kindness and discuss examples of how students' interactions might play out in the classroom.

RUDENESS

Reflection Questions

When a child is selfish or rude, the stern voice of my mother echoes in my ears, "Excuse me, young lady . . . just who do you think you are?" She made it clear that being selfish or curt was not acceptable in our family. My mom taught me that it felt good to be kind. When I was kind, I could see that others felt good too. She told me that kindness is a sign of pride in myself and appreciation of others.

Some of the comments that young students utter in frustration or ignorance are slight and mumbled under their breath, and some comments are boldly stated and meant to hurt outright. Either way, looking at the particular situations

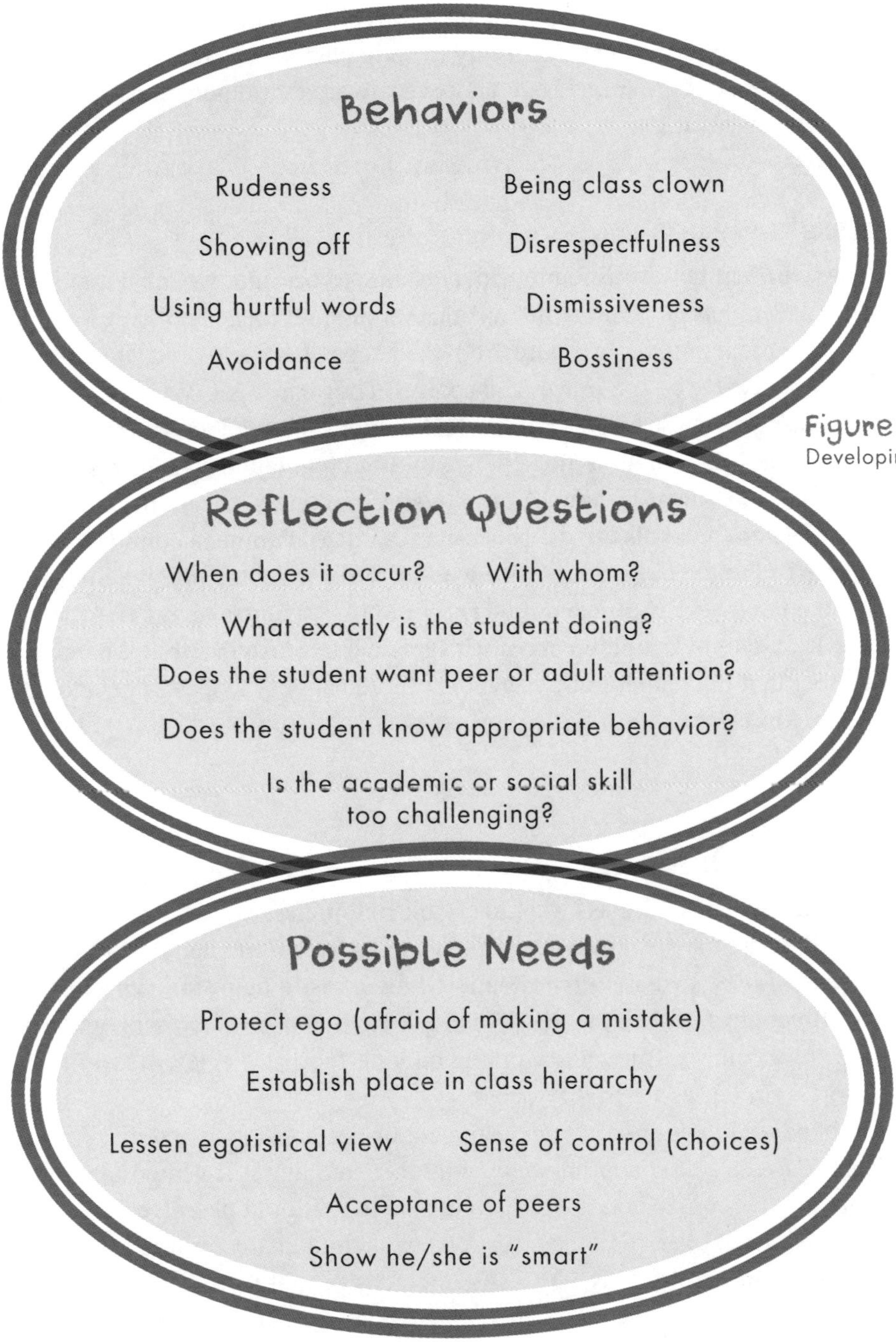

Behaviors

Rudeness	Being class clown
Showing off	Disrespectfulness
Using hurtful words	Dismissiveness
Avoidance	Bossiness

Figure 7.2
Developing Kindness

Reflection Questions

When does it occur?   With whom?

What exactly is the student doing?

Does the student want peer or adult attention?

Does the student know appropriate behavior?

Is the academic or social skill
too challenging?

Possible Needs

Protect ego (afraid of making a mistake)

Establish place in class hierarchy

Lessen egotistical view   Sense of control (choices)

Acceptance of peers

Show he/she is "smart"

can help us. Are the comments constant or directed at one child? Are children being rude to their classmates as a way to be in charge? Do they think their snappy comebacks are funny? Are they even aware that others find their comments unsettling?

Possible Needs

To help children get comfortable with choosing to be kind, we must make it a priority to emphasize positive interactions throughout the school day. Young children are reacting, biologically, from the needs of security and survival, affection and esteem, and power and control. They can easily be overwhelmed by the duality of these impulses. Do I feel safe or do I need to protect myself? Do I feel connected or am I alone? The ability to regulate these desires does not develop in a linear fashion and can overlap and even regress throughout the early years (Nuckols 2010). This can mean that Jasmine is confident and in charge of Puppy Tag at recess one week and insecure and pouting on the bench the next week. Sulimann might share during science lab on Tuesday but on Thursday he's arguing about who gets the microscope first. We must remember that our students are navigating these slippery slopes of development and offer kindness as a consistent cornerstone when they are feeling vulnerable or confused.

Possible Actions

Some students in every class want to establish dominance or power in a group setting. Research suggests that they likely are seeking a momentary sense of control in lives that are often chaotic. My work is to help students gain long-term control of their emotions so they can feel empowered without trying to overpower others. But while working on long-term strategies, we can't ignore the short-term lapses when they occur.

Whenever I hear or see a rude comment or gesture, I stop and make the student redo the action appropriately, right then and there. It's important to consistently recognize good behavior but also to point out negative behaviors so children don't ever think they can get away with hurtful comments in our classroom community. I say, "You will not talk like that to your friend. Try it again." I then will ask the other student to explain how the comment felt so that the perpetrator can directly connect the action to the feelings. I end the talk with, "Your friends like you; they don't like when you act this way. They are trying to help you be a better friend."

When we point out these behaviors, on a large or small scale, to the whole class we establish the expected style of behaving toward one another. (After several similar lessons, the teacher's legendary raised eyebrow and incredulous stare usually do the trick.)

Sometimes students learn a sassy comment or gesture from the older brothers and sisters in a family. An eighth-grade comment such as "Dude, you stink at basketball" might be a joke among thirteen-year-old boys, but most seven-year-olds are not yet capable of interpreting such comments as jokes and will consider them personal attacks instead. Be sure to stop all comments even if the students plead that they were just joking or claim, "We say it at home all the time." I explain that while they may say such things outside school, inside school we don't talk to one another disrespectfully.

UNDERSTANDING THE ROLE OF KINDNESS IN THE CLASSROOM COMMUNITY

Reflection Questions

Families have varied ways of handling chores and responsibilities, such as cleaning the table after eating, sorting dirty clothes, and picking up toys after playing. Families also have different ways of communicating. When children act unkindly at school, we must consider the context of their actions. Do a child's family members take notice when a friend picks up a coat from the floor, or do they let everyone "trash" the house without consequences? Do a child's parents always let her go first on the swing set, or do they ask her to take turns and be courteous to others? Does a student realize when someone has given him a compliment, or do his family members speak harshly at home?

If respect and courtesy are not part of some students' upbringing, we will have to teach those skills with more scaffolding and nuance. For example, we might need to stress the cause and effect of actions, such as explaining how cleaning up together helps the class get to recess sooner.

Possible Needs

Some children come to school with little understanding of what it means to be kind. It's not that they are mean at heart, but they seem to have little recognition of the action or know how to show genuine kindness to others. I remember Carlos, a small, quiet, and attentive student in my kindergarten class. When it was cleanup time, Carlos would move about the room chatting with friends, looking busy and helpful, when in fact he was not cleaning up anything. He moved cheerfully from blocks to art center to puzzles, never once picking up a brush or a Lego block. As I watched him I did not see defiance or mischief; Carlos just did not see that he had a role in keeping our classroom in order.

I had used the Responsive Classroom technique of Interactive Modeling to teach the classroom procedures of pushing in their chairs. I explained that, with twenty-three chairs in the room, we would need to keep them neat in order to be safe. I modeled getting up from a chair and how to push it in. I then had three students model the same behavior and we discussed what we noticed as a class: "Edwin was walking," "Jennifer stopped so she didn't bump into Kenny," and "Raymond made sure the chair was all the way under the table." We connected those actions with being safe and kind. ("When the chairs are all the way under, no one will trip. That's kind.") Then eight children modeled the procedures, then twelve, and then all twenty-three of us readily modeled how to push in our chairs and keep the room orderly.

That is, everyone but Carlos. He cheerfully joined the group and enjoyed the drama aspect of the lesson but never once pushed in a chair! Again, his behavior did not reflect defiance or noncompliance; he truly did not connect his actions to his environment or to the people around him.

Was my implementation of the lesson not explicit enough? Maybe I introduced too many routines too soon. Maybe Carlos was from a family that did not require him to take responsibility. What was it that Carlos needed to become fully invested in our community? I reflected on his behavior, and a pattern emerged.

During recess, Carlos would play tag with the others but would run just outside the playing field so he never got caught. At center time he would build a structure next to his friends and share the blocks, but his fantasy dialogue did not match the story line of his friends (and his story usually included total destruction of the creation, frustrating his friends). During Reading Workshop he would sit next to his reading buddy and animatedly tell the story, but he held the book tight to his lap, peering at the illustrations, never noticing that his partner could not see the pictures. He was kind, not aggressive or domineering; he was simply immature and unaware of others in general. He seemed oblivious to his friends' wants or feelings.

Because I taught Carlos before I had fully implemented Friendship Workshops into my classroom, I worked with him individually, helping him identify facial and body languages as the starting point for developing compassion for others. During guided reading, Carlos and I spent a lot of time discussing the characters and how they were kind. In writing I would occasionally coauthor a story with Carlos, one that focused on a real-life event from the playground in order to emphasize his connection to his classmates. I would elicit Carlos's direct help in organizing the writing materials and then publicly thank him for being kind later during Writing Workshop.

Slowly, oh so slowly, Carlos made progress. At the end of the school year I reflected on Carlos's transformation by using our chair lesson as a symbolic example. Carlos started out the year having no idea that he was responsible for the chair. His involvement with it was temporary and when he was finished using it, it ceased to exist. After several weeks of reminders and one-on-one practice, Carlos one day walked away from the table, took a few steps, and then stopped. He looked back at the chair and then at me. "Is that chair not safe?" he asked. He genuinely was unsure of the answer, but he had become aware of things outside his egocentric circle. He was starting to put the pieces together.

Months later, I observed Carlos passing by another student's chair, which had not been properly stowed. "Ms. Buckley, that chair is not under the table," he said loudly. "You are right, Carlos," I said. "It shouldn't be out there." Carlos smiled and shook his head . . . and walked away. It made me chuckle because while he had grown into recognizing the "mistake," he still did not recognize that he had the ability to fix it.

Sometime in late spring I watched Carlos and Giselle working together at math time. When it was time to clean up they gathered the math cubes and started to put them away in the math shelves. As Giselle walked away, Carlos said, "Giselle, your chair. It's supposed to go under, right?" "Oh yeah," she said. "Thanks, Carlos." Carlos pushed the chair under the table and I heard him quietly say to himself, "I pushed in the chair." The grin on his face filled my heart with pride!

There were other similar examples of Carlos's development that year. He learned he could work *with* his friends and be a part of the learning. He would join them at blocks, and instead of clashing story lines, he would offer suggestions and extend the plot. These stories often carried over into Writing Workshop where Carlos could now focus for thirty minutes on his illustrations and words.

Carlos eventually learned to share the materials more easily because he trusted that his friends would use the materials respectfully and return them to the correct places. This allowed the class to work with the magnifying glasses at the science table, the headphones at the listening center, and the Unifix cubes at math stations cooperatively so I could work with small groups for extended periods of time.

Carlos also learned to compromise with his friends. He would ask Sulimann to swing with him at recess, and when Sulimann wanted to play tag instead, Carlos would agree, saying, "Tag today, swings tomorrow, okay?" This skill transferred into Carlos's listening to other ideas during science talks, accepting different ways to solve a math story problem, and asking questions when he didn't understand our read-aloud.

When Bryan joined our classroom in February, it was Carlos who showed him the ropes. Carlos walked with Bryan to lunch and explained the cafeteria rules of staying in your seat. Carlos chose Bryan for his reading buddy and taught him all our songs and poems. He showed Bryan where to hang his wet paintings and how to clean up the paint area. Through repeated and explicit lessons on kindness, Carlos grew into a courteous and helpful member of our community.

Possible Actions

Some children will need very explicit lessons on what kindness is and when it occurs. One way to stress this is to make simple picture books with photographs of their friends being kind. Point out when other people are kind to them and be sure they say, "Thank you." My colleague Emelie Parker would purposely drop a handful of markers on the ground near the student and say, "Oh, would you be kind and help me pick these up?" (And, being Emelie, she would sneak in some counting skills too!)

I developed a sticker one year that said, "I was kind today." At the end of the day we would join for a closing circle and reflect on how the day went. I started the year off by telling students when I saw them being kind and giving them a sticker. After a month, I asked if anyone could identify a time they were kind to someone else. And another month later, I asked if anyone could identify when someone was kind to them. The student talking would then hand the sticker to the other person and say, "Thank you for being kind." Finally I asked them if they could leave themselves out of it, so to speak, and identify when a classmate was kind to someone else. Eventually the students started giving the sticker to one another at random parts of the day when they saw kind behavior.

ATTENTION-GETTING DISTRACTIONS

Reflection Questions

Many disruptive behaviors are really pleas for attention. Does the student need recognition or acceptance from peers or adults? Is she seeking encouragement, assistance to build more stamina to complete assignments, or distraction from the task? If the latter, does she feel confused about the purpose or perhaps overwhelmed by the number of required steps? How can we make it comfortable for her to continue? We might also consider whether the behavior is situational. How does she interact in purely social situations (the playground, after school) versus in math groups or as a writing research partner?

Possible Needs

Many students looking for adult attention do not care whether the attention is positive or negative; they just want attention! It is easy for teachers to fall into the habit of reprimanding students for negative behavior, only to find they have reinforced the behavior because it gave them what they wanted.

Possible Actions

Providing individual attention to every student is impossible every day. But there are ways to help students feel more connected, even special, in large classrooms. One way is to set up a Lunch Bunch group. Decide on the frequency (once a week, once a month) and allow the child to invite a friend to eat in the classroom with you while the other students eat in the cafeteria. This is easy because it requires no planning or prep work, no materials or documentation chart. It is an enjoyable thirty minutes of connecting and (usually) laughing. Quietly mentioning a Lunch Buddy joke or conversation during the regular school routine can start to satisfy students' need for attention and encourage them to give others compliments as well.

LEARNING TO TRUST

Reflection Questions

Trust, reliability, and truth are critical to healthy relationships, but these qualities are even more important to teachers and students. When students do not feel that these qualities are in place, they can become self-protective and combative. Don't engage in a blame game as you investigate the causes. Think like a detective by asking, Is trust an issue? Does the student question every decision you make? Does he challenge other teachers as well? Is he reacting to the actual decision or to authority in general? Does he change his stories when confronted with his misbehavior? Has he shown small improvements in accepting responsibility?

Possible Needs

Megan Tschannen-Moran, the author of *Trust Matters: Leadership for Successful Schools*, defines trust as "one's willingness to be vulnerable to another based on the confidence that the other is benevolent, honest, open, reliable, and competent" (2004, xiii). Consistency is a key factor in helping build trust, truthfulness, and reliability. Every time we demonstrate these qualities, through our smiles, our attentive listening, and our firm rules, young children feel safe and protected and become willing to take risks in their relationships and their learning.

Possible Actions

There is a time and place for obedience and silence—the Westminster Dog Show! Okay, okay, it is true there are times when students need to be quiet and follow the rules without discussion, but they will be more likely to comply if we give them choices and some control at other times during the school day. For example, research has shown that students are less likely to engage in tattling and fighting when they can make some of the decisions about learning (Denton 2005).

I remember my brother, Kent, sharing a piece of parenting wisdom with me when he saw that my son would throw a tantrum whenever I made him eat peas at dinnertime. "Offer Griffin peas or carrots," Kent suggested. "Don't offer him peas or jelly beans with the hopes he will choose the peas; he won't. It's really about eating *some* vegetable, not specifically peas, right?"

Whether we say the Pledge of Allegiance before or after taking the lunch count or which book we read first at Reading Workshop are inconsequential to me—both events will happen, and both are good for the students. So why not let them decide? When students get to make some of the "important" decisions for our classroom, they are more willing to trust me and each other. Find ways to offer your class small choices every day.

A common question asked in schools is "Are you making a good decision right now?" Children don't learn to make decisions by obeying but by trying, sometimes failing, and then trying again. When you know the science center is a popular choice at indoor recess, offer students a choice for sharing the hand lenses: Do they want to set the timer for fifteen minutes or do they want to use the bell? I know some classes have established a rule that small decisions like that would be handled by using the game Rock, Paper, Scissors and everyone agrees to live by the outcome. Allowing the student to choose which math worksheet to complete (both involve practicing multiplication, so the required skill remains the same) or where to sit during independent reading are small ways to begin building trust with students.

KINDNESS IS AS KINDNESS DOES

The Greek philosopher Aristotle is quoted as saying, "Educating the mind without educating the heart is no education at all." We have strict curriculum requirements filling our lesson plan books, incessant deadlines filling our calendars, and numerous benchmarks filling our progress reports. But most important, we have young people filling our classrooms. They are searching to connect, understand, and contribute. The diversity of our schools and our nation means that our workplaces will be filled with different cultures, languages, and experiences. Our students need the ability to communicate and collaborate in those environments, and we must teach them the skills that will enable them to be successful.

The Partnership for 21st Century Skills reminds us that "Mutually beneficial relationships are a central undercurrent to accomplishments in businesses. . . . All Americans must be skilled at interacting competently and respectfully with others" (2008, 10). Learning to communicate with kindness and respect allows all voices to be heard, all ideas to grow, and all people to succeed. Classrooms that foster kindness can provide students with the safety and security they need to become creative writers, inspired scientists, and innovative mathematicians while embodying tolerance, acceptance, and compassion for others.

Chapter 8

PEACEFULNESS

Children who have been exposed to violence (either personally or because they have seen others being hurt) become fearful, anxious, and reactionary. Often they do not know what triggered the violence, so they are on guard and never feel safe. Some shut down and find it difficult to trust others or learn from them. Others may imitate the intimidation and verbal and physical abuse from home when dealing with peers.

Fortunately, most of our students have loving support at home and do not have anger-based reactions in the classroom. But I suspect that all teachers have had students who cower or cause others to cower because of the trauma they have suffered. Recall from Chapter 2 what happens to the brain under stress. People have strong physical and emotional reactions to perceived threats, whether or not the challenges are real. The student who fears giving the wrong answer or who becomes frustrated after one mistake may be feeling insecure, anxious, or defensive. Understanding the effects of fear helps me empathize with students who are easily irritated or distraught.

Calming down is a Friendship Workshop lesson that is easy to relate to as a teacher. As adults, we try to release stress almost every day. How many times have you closed your eyes for just a brief moment when little Travis was headed your way, in tears, again? How many times have you held your breath in amazement as Yasmine threw food in the cafeteria, again? And my personal favorite, how many times did I place my hand gently (but oh so firmly) on Jack's shoulder and say, "DUDE [in breath] Stooooooop [out breath]." (Answer: a bazillion.)

From my meditation practice I have experienced firsthand the mental benefits of methodically following my breath. The physical benefits of rhythmic breathing are significant as well. There is consistent evidence that incorporating routine short breaks of rhythmic breathing can lower aggression levels, lower blood pressure, and regulate the heart rate. Across all grade levels, schools around the country have reported higher attendance rates, fewer suspensions, and higher standardized test scores after instituting short, systematic meditation programs (Nidich et al. 2011).

PRACTICING PEACE

The class gathers in a circle and I begin the lesson with a personal example. Perhaps my son was playing ball in the house—after I told him not to—and a bowl breaks. Or maybe someone cut in front of me at the drive-up bank window after I had been waiting in line for twenty-five minutes. The story itself is not important, but revealing a personal time when I "lost it" eases the children's worries that it is wrong to feel angry. I am sure to include what my face looked like, what my body felt like, and what I wanted to do (ram my car into his car) but didn't. I ask for other examples from the children's experiences and they model what their faces looked like, how their bodies felt, what they "really, really" wanted to do.

After describing the situation that made me angry I explain that I did not like how my body felt. The tension in my shoulders hurt my back, the tightness in my jaws gave me a headache, and the frustration made me want to cry. I explain that before I can act better I need to feel better. So I share with them a simple breathing method of calming myself down. We start with our palms faceup by our sides. We take a slow, deep breath in through our noses as our hands gently float upward to our shoulders. As we begin to slowly exhale through our mouths, we turn our hands to face palms down and gently float them back down to our sides. We do this three times and feel our bodies relax and our minds become peaceful. Now we are more capable of fixing a problem.

I use this technique when we have a special visitor coming in, or the day before Valentine's Day, or when we've just seen the first snowfall—anytime the energy in the classroom is palpable and edgy. Other calming techniques include counting backward from ten, humming a simple song three times, or taking ten giant steps away from the situation. Allow your class to find its own unique ways to actively feel better. A simple poster makes a good reference, or anchor chart, for students to refer to when they need support.

The calming techniques are helpful when trying to shift the emotions at the moment, but sometimes students aren't sure what feelings to substitute instead. In other words, they don't really know what peacefulness *feels* like. Besides read-alouds, I use art as a means of defining peacefulness, giving students a better understanding and more specific vocabulary to identify emotions. Next, I focus on the inner sense of happiness. Not the "I got a new toy from Kmart yesterday" kind of happy but the deeper sense of being at ease within our bodies. I choose the word *peaceful*, but I am sure any word that resonates with you would work, such as *calm, happy, quiet, safe,* and so on.

As a group we look at art prints and identify what is in the picture, what feelings the art stirs in us, and why we think those feelings are there. I model for the class how to share ideas about art with a partner. (Over the years I have collected and laminated dozens of pieces from galleries and museums, but you may find it easier to print items you find through Internet searches on cardstock and place them in plastic sleeves. Check for copyright issues.)

THE ART OF EMOTIONS

Scarlett and I sit side by side and look at Ansel Adams's print, *Fresh Snow, Yosemite Valley, California,* taken in 1947 (Figure 8.1 is a similar print).

I ask her what she sees in the print. "I see snow on the trees." (It will take time to get past the surface ideas.)

"Me too," I say. "I like snow. It's always so clean looking before people walk on it."

"Once, me and my dad went walking at night when it was snowing," Scarlett shares. "It was so quiet. You could see it but couldn't hear it."

Bingo! Scarlett nailed it! "I've done that too, and you're right, it is quiet. That's what peaceful could sound like, isn't it?"

"Yeah, quiet as soft snow drifting down." (Scarlett is our wanna-be poet, always has a beautiful phrase up her sleeve.)

Figure 8.1
Photographs like this one help start our discussion of what peacefulness feels and sounds like.

© 2012 Larry Lamsa

As I debrief the lesson with the class I point out that Scarlett and I made a personal connection to the print. Neither of us had ever been to Yosemite National Park, but we have seen and felt the joy of a new snowfall. In sharing our thoughts and reactions, we unravel what peacefulness means to us as individuals. We then partner with a classmate and look at a variety of prints to see if they make us feel calm. We repeat this exercise for several days with different prints and different partners. After several rounds of observing and discussing, students choose a print to laminate as a bookmark for them to keep in their book boxes.

Christy Hermann Thompson's class made a book for their classroom library titled *Peace Can Be. . . .* It had the art print, a photo of each student, and a speech bubble explaining why the print made them feel peaceful. Christy and the class pulled that book out at least once a semester and giggled at how their faces or their handwriting had changed. But more important, it was a quiet reminder of how it feels to be peaceful inside.

I also use music to develop a sense of peacefulness. For example, children easily tune in to the fact that William Ackerman's acoustic guitar physically stirs up different sensations and images than Tchaikovsky's *1812 Overture*. These lessons give us more insights about our emotions and develop a more extensive vocabulary for expressing them. Learning words such as *graceful* and *serene* or *excited* and *agitated* help students understand the complexity of their emotions. Using music and paintings also creates the framework for future literacy work such as predicting, inferring, and referring to the work to confirm their answers. Through this process, the children also come to understand that liking different things is okay and makes us interesting and fun to be with.

LEARNING TO REST

Every day, whether I am teaching kindergarten or second grade, my class stops for ten minutes and rests. Everyone, including me and the assistant teacher, is required to sit or lie down on the floor in a comfortable position and just be; no talking, no reading, no drawing. I put on quiet music and we just sit. It only takes a few weeks in September to establish this as a normal part of our day. I must admit, I do it more for me than the kids, but they quickly (if only unconsciously) enjoy the benefits, too. My chosen time is usually after recess, and it allows us a smooth transition into the afternoon's work. Some teachers have said they don't have ten minutes to spare, but I figure if I am feeling like that, then that's exactly when I need ten minutes of downtime—and my students probably do, too.

CULTIVATING PEACEFULNESS

Figure 8.2 shows a graphic representation of the reflective process that I go through as I consider the possible causes of students' misbehaviors, observe their interpersonal relationships, and think of actions I could take to address their social and emotional needs in terms of peacefulness and then to redirect their behavior. In the following section, I explore different sets of teacher reflections related to the Friendship Workshop topic of peacefulness and discuss examples of how students' interactions might play out in the classroom.

Reflection Questions

The first and most obvious question to ask is "Who is the flare-up happening with?" So often children get stuck in a pattern of behavior toward certain individuals—the phrase *like oil and water* comes to mind. Is the student

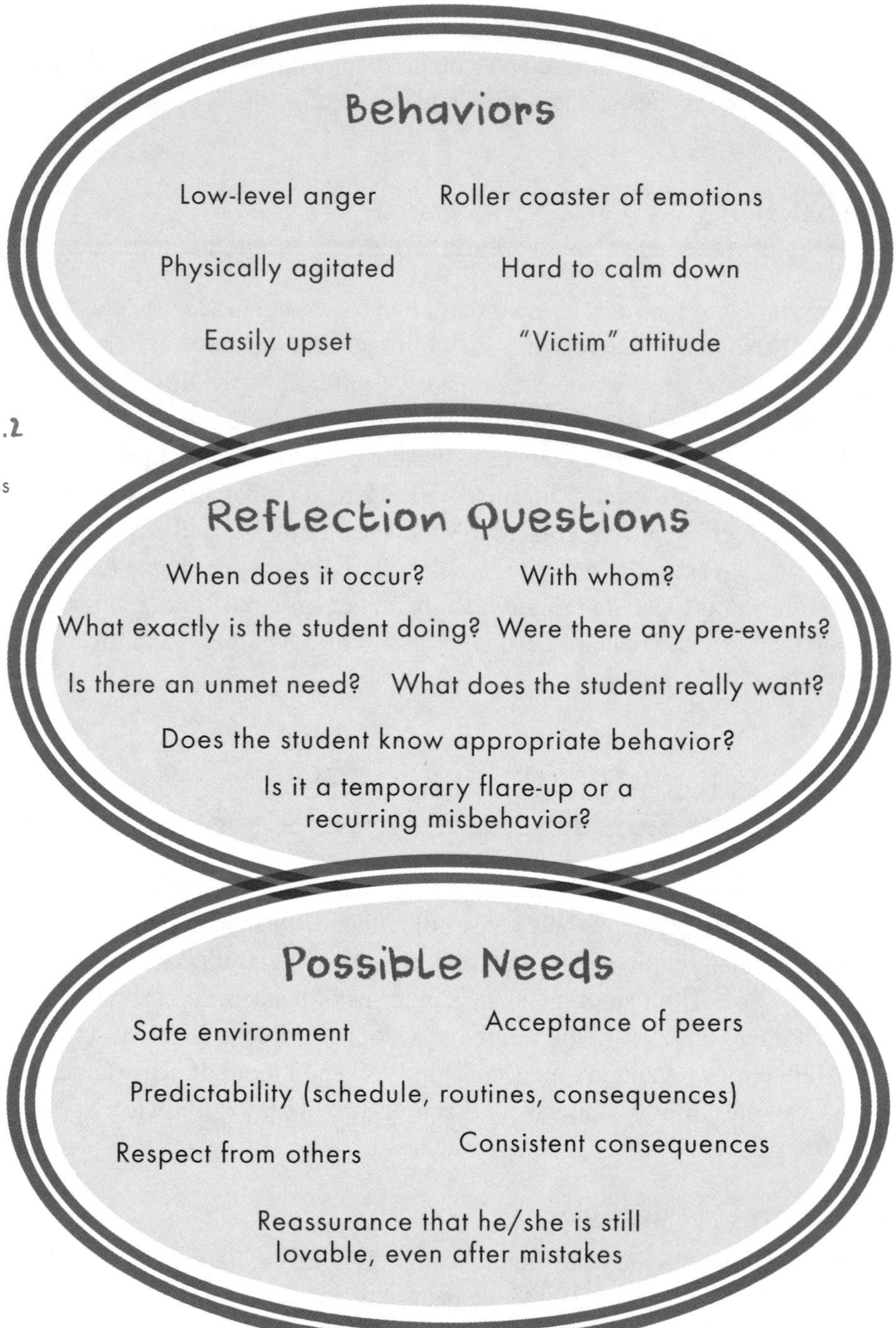

Behaviors

Low-level anger   Roller coaster of emotions

Physically agitated   Hard to calm down

Easily upset   "Victim" attitude

Figure 8.2
Developing
Peacefulness

Reflection Questions

When does it occur?   With whom?

What exactly is the student doing?   Were there any pre-events?

Is there an unmet need?   What does the student really want?

Does the student know appropriate behavior?

Is it a temporary flare-up or a
recurring misbehavior?

Possible Needs

Safe environment   Acceptance of peers

Predictability (schedule, routines, consequences)

Respect from others   Consistent consequences

Reassurance that he/she is still
lovable, even after mistakes

misbehaving toward one or two individuals? Does she lash out only when she is in line with Scarlett, or does she feel annoyed when she is physically close to anybody? Does she have moments of working appropriately throughout the day?

PERSONAL SPACE

Possible Needs

During the early weeks of school, students are just beginning to learn how to move and control their bodies in the small space of the classroom. Bumps, nudges, pokes, and brushes happen frequently, and young children tend to react spontaneously and impulsively because they believe they were hurt deliberately. Their reactions usually stem from feeling powerless or helpless, and the physical response can seem to be the most immediate way to remedy their discomfort.

Possible Actions

Understanding each person's need for personal space can be a difficult concept for young students to grasp. If they are standing there, then it's *their* personal space! Friendship Workshop lessons focusing on how to sit next to someone on the carpet without knees banging or how to stand in line without elbows bashing are simple but important. Some teachers call it "bubble space," asking students to imagine a large floating bubble around them that will pop if it's too close to someone else. (Of course, you then have to deal with the jokester who sneakily pretends to pop everyone's bubble!)

Other basic lessons include having two students move about the classroom without touching anything or anyone, then incrementally increasing the number of students in the orbit while the others notice and discuss what is happening. I use Focus Five Inc.'s (www.artsintegrationconsulting.com) "Actor's Toolbox" to teach students about concentration, cooperation, and collaboration while strengthening their sense of both personal and group space. The students gather silently in a circle as the music starts. We reach down to our toes and say, "I control my body [as we slowly draw our hands up to our necks], and my voice [as we quietly breathe out and touch our throats] and my mind [as we gently touch our temples]. I use my imagination [as we gently pull our hands away from our temples] to concentrate [as we lift our arms above our heads] and cooperate [as we slowly and gently place them on the back of the people standing on either side of us]." In the beginning, we use the words to describe the motions, but eventually we are silent throughout the activity. The Focus Five workshop is straightforward, relevant, and energizing and I highly recommend it.

CLARIFYING RULES AND PROCEDURES

Reflection Question

Does the student feel safe in the classroom? Does he know the routines and procedures for starting the day? For cleaning up? Do I take the time to clearly explain the day's schedule and answer any questions? Are there places in the room that allow children to work away from the crowd?

Possible Needs

A safe environment is the second tier of Maslow's Hierarchy. One aspect of a safe classroom environment is ensuring that students feel secure and confident in the routines and procedures throughout the day. Unexpected changes can heighten their anxiety. Their need for predictability may be their way of buffering stress that happens at home or between friends or in the cafeteria line. Feeling certain of their environment enables them to relax.

Possible Actions

A predictable schedule gives consistency to students' days, creates a sense of control, and provides an internal sense of safety. An individual class schedule on each child's desk can be helpful for students to mark off as events occur. We can laminate them so the students can fill in the blank schedule each morning to help solidify their understanding of the day's events, then wipe it clean the next day and start over. Having a designated buddy to check in with when transitions are taking place can also offset a student's anxiety. The buddy can provide verbal support, telling the student what is next, or she can help the student gather materials for the next lesson.

Some students may benefit from having their own designated space slightly away from their peers. A first grader in Melissa Fleischer's class needed some seclusion, so Melissa used colorful tape and accessories to create "Dylan's Office." Melissa added lines on the floor and the countertop and placed all the materials Dylan would need throughout the day within arm's reach. With the class she discussed that no one was allowed in Dylan's office unless he invited them. The discussion was honest and respectful and gave Dylan the time and space to develop his interpersonal skills of cooperating and collaborating.

IDENTIFYING THE TRIGGERS

Reflection Questions

Watch to see what is happening right before the student's outburst. Does he react at certain times of the day or on certain days? Is it really "all of a sudden," or can you see signs of smoldering frustration growing?

What was the student trying to accomplish before the outburst? If the fight concerns the right to use the blue crayon, we know that there are almost always other crayons to use instead. Is it more likely that the student feels crowded and needs space to work? Could it be that the student is easily frustrated and has poor time management skills, meaning that he can't pause to color the trees green now while waiting for the blue crayon that will let him finish the skyline?

Possible Needs

When students act out in anger they are sometimes trying to gain control but can't identify the core problem because their emotions are too high. Their need to be right or vindicated can override their ability to act appropriately. When students feel they are being wronged, their emotions can begin to cascade into one another. Irritation flows into resentment, which flows into anger, and suddenly they are inconsolable. They need to be able to calm down and slow down before they can address the situation.

Possible Actions

Calming techniques such as breathing slowly, counting to ten, and other soothing practices can help release the tension and slow the adrenaline flow so students can explain the situation peacefully. (See Figure 8.3 for an example of a calming-down poster.) A small bucket filled with rice to drag their hands through or a large thick rubber band to pull on can provide students with a more tangible method of defusing their intense emotions. A short walk to a nearby classroom to run an errand can help them regain self-control and feel safe enough to problem solve with a peer. (I'm sure all teachers have their own version of this—such as writing a message in cursive, which is indecipherable to most students these days, to the teacher in a nearby classroom that says, "Help! We both need a break!")

Learn to recognize the signs of students who have angry flare-ups so you can be proactive. When starting a new project that requires cooperation, for example, assign yourself to the group with the person who has a shorter fuse. If your art class involves a fine-motor skill project, ask the student if he wants help cutting out shapes. If you see a student get left out on the playground, wander over and ask about her new puppy. Sometimes giving students a chance to take a break and talk about something unrelated but pleasant, such as a recent family outing, is all that they need to change their unsettled mind-set and relax.

Figure 8.3
A simple poster made during Friendship Workshop reminds students of three ways to calm down.

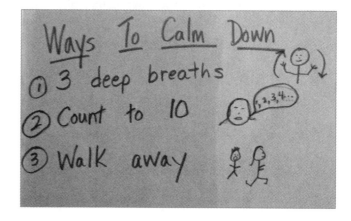

PLAYING THE VICTIM ROLE

Reflection Questions

Does the student constantly blame a specific child? Has she developed a "victim" attitude when explaining a problem (meaning she only sees how she was wronged in a situation)? Listen carefully to the words children use when describing their experience. Are they regularly saying, "He *always* ____ to me" or "She *never* ____ with me"?

Possible Needs

Developmentally, a child's brain from the ages of two to ten is generally incapable of self-reflection. The brain takes in information, records the cause and effect, and calculates the results as absolutes (Nuckols 2010). In this egotistical realm, children typically see others as the cause of their unhappiness. They do not yet have the ability to see their role in creating or contributing to a problem. They need to learn that there are always two points of view, which may be in conflict.

Possible Actions

Addressing a disagreement does not mean solving the problem for the children; that is how teachers end up with a group of tattletales and whiners. Addressing means giving each child time to explain his point of view, identify the root of the problem, and agree on a solution that respects both parties. At the beginning of the year, I stop the entire class and go through these steps for the smallest infractions. When Abigail whines, "She never shares stamps with me; only with Giselle," or Jeffrey complains, "No, you can't play here. You always knock over my tower," I stop the class and bring the two students together.

"Jeffrey, you sound very upset with Nabeel. Can you tell me why?"

When Jeffrey starts to say, "He always . . ." I immediately stop him. "Let's use Nabeel's name and let's only talk about what happened right now. So try this: I was building when Nabeel . . ."

Jeffrey explains that he was building and Nabeel poked his foot at the base of the tower and it started to wobble, but then Nabeel bursts in with, "No, I did not!" Again I immediately stop the talk.

"Nabeel, it is Jeffrey's turn to talk. He's going to explain what happened and we are going to listen to hear how Jeffrey is feeling. You will explain your side next and we will listen to how you are feeling, okay?" Nabeel nods reluctantly but knows he will get his turn.

When both boys have finished their explanations, it is clear that while Nabeel tried to make his toe poke seem like an accident, it really wasn't. So first, we discuss how he needs to control all parts of his body when walking. Then we discuss how much Nabeel likes Jeffrey's building skills, and I ask if he would like to learn how to build a tunnel. His big brown eyes light up.

"So, what do you think the real problem was?" I ask the boys.

"That Nabeel didn't tell me he wanted to build with me," offers Jeffrey.

"That I didn't ask Jeffrey to help me build a tunnel," says Nabeel.

"So tell me if I got this right," I say, summarizing. "Jeffrey was building a cool tower, and Nabeel, you wanted to learn how to build a tunnel but didn't know how to ask. Am I right so far?" The boys agree. "So Nabeel inched his toe near the base of the tower to pretend to knock it over, right?" Sheepishly Nabeel nods his head yes. "But what did you really want to do, Nabeel? You wanted to ask Jeffrey . . ."

"If he could help me build a tunnel."

"That's right. When we like something someone can do, like build a tower or read a book, we can ask, 'Will you help me?' Would that have let Jeffrey build his tower and you a tunnel?"

Affirmative head nods.

"Okay," I say. "Let's try it right now."

I send Jeffrey back to the blocks and he starts building his tower. Nabeel and I wander over, and I tell Nabeel to poke his toe like he did earlier and then I stop him with grand, dramatic flair: "Wait! Stop! What can you do instead, Nabeel?"

Holding back the giggles, Nabeel says, "Jeffrey, can you help me build a tunnel?" and Jeffrey replies, "Sure" and the two spend the last eight minutes of center time working together.

Stopping the entire class ensures that everyone learns the procedures for how we handle disputes. As the months pass, I tend to resolve disputes with the aggrieved students only when they indicate chronic problems. If only a few students are struggling with remembering to use the process, I will offer support as long as needed. Most students feel empowered by not needing an adult to solve their disputes. I wean myself away from being the mediator, and the students simply tell me the solution (and I give double high fives, bear hugs, and other rave reviews for being so strong and kind!).

CONSISTENT CONSEQUENCES

Reflection Questions

Every student worries about the consequences after misbehaving. Have I established clear and obvious consequences to the students? Do they feel secure in knowing which offenses are small and uncomplicated and which are serious? Or do I change the consequences depending on my mood, patience level, or time frame (gulp . . . guilty . . .)?

Possible Needs

Students want to know the consequences for misdeeds but, more important, they need to know exactly how they will be treated after making a mistake. They may not mind getting a period of time-out or having to draw what they should have done, but they can become very worried about how we will perceive them after they admit to a mistake. A small misdeed can become a larger classroom issue if students do not feel safe enough to admit their wrongdoings.

A student who is easily upset or irritated is especially prone to anxiety and will deny the truth to the bitter end, rather than face an unknown penalty. I saw this when Maria pushed Jessica too hard on the swing. Now Jessica is standing in front of me in tears, with a small scrape on her knee.

"Did you push Jessica, Maria?" I ask. Slow head shake, indicating no. (Okay, I think to myself. Let's start simple.)

"Did you push Jessica on the swings?" I ask more specifically. Again the no. (Oh, she's going to be a tough nut to crack. I better start at the very beginning.)

"I saw you and Jessica playing together. Was it fun?" I ask, trying a third time. A muffled "Yes" comes from Maria's teary face. (All right, she can tell the truth. Now I'm getting somewhere!)

"Were you two taking turns pushing each other on the swing?" Another muffled "Yes."

"Was Jessica on the swing?" Maria nods her head yes. (Still telling the truth, a good sign.)

"Did you push Jessica too hard, Maria?" I ask. A determined head shake no and we are back where we started. (I can see my recess is over.)

Sometimes when students act out repeatedly in small ways, it may be to test the teacher. They may doubt their ability or their own self-worth and seek validation through misbehavior. They may try to trap you in a tedious exchange in order to avoid work and test your limits. In these instances, it is important to use language that reinforces it was the mistake that was inappropriate, not the student himself. *The Power of Our Words* by Paula Denton (2007) outlines the three Rs for teacher language: Reinforcing, Reminding, and Redirecting. Using a peaceful tone of voice and calm body language and being as succinct as possible ("Stop talking and raise your hand if you have a question" instead of "Mario, how many times do I have to tell you to not shout out?") keeps the focus on the behavior while supporting the student with peaceful alternatives.

Possible Actions

I have had students over the years who came from homes where abuse was present, and for these students my positive and predictable responses in the classroom became healing balms. Yet from my research, I discovered that even students from safe and loving homes benefit from knowing that their teachers will not shout at them, spank them, or hit them. Hearing that they are safe even when they have misbehaved is soothing and can help them admit mistakes. Reassure students that mistakes in the classroom are expected and normal and are always handled with honesty and caring. I model apologizing and forgiving in my daily interactions.

When I am demonstrating how to cut a piece of construction paper for a class project, I purposely make a mistake and say, "Oh, man! I ruined it. I should just give up!" Then I flop my hands and scissors down and give my best pouty face. The children always (and I mean always) jump to my defense:

"No, no, don't. You can fix it. Try this . . ." I look up. "You mean it's okay I made a mistake?" Heads nod encouragingly. "I can try again?" More heads nod. "Okay, so what can I try to fix my mistake, Yancy?" Children are instinctively kind and want to make others feel good. Modeling the appropriate vocabulary and actions when emotions are low can set up successful exchanges later when circumstances get trickier.

LITERACY CONNECTIONS: KINDNESS AND PEACEFULNESS CONNECT TO ASKING QUESTIONS, LISTENING FOR ANSWERS, AND WRITING WORDLESS PICTURE BOOKS

In the weeks following our Friendship Workshop lessons about kindness and peacefulness, we continue to share stories, and now the children, who feel safe and equipped with the tools needed to communicate their feelings and calm themselves down, begin to take command of the storytelling chair during Writing Workshop. They are eager to share their stories of birthdays and Christmases, of baby brothers and special cousins, of bowling or seeing the Easter Bunny at the mall. We feel accepted when we hear a story that is similar to ours and practice using kind words when making comments and connecting to the feelings within the stories.

Talking, Drawing, Writing: Lessons for Our Youngest Writers by Martha Horn and Mary Ellen Giacobbe (2007) is a fabulous book that explains the power of storytelling and how to use it to support early writing work. The words and tones the authors use with their young writers lets the children know they are already capable authors. As I call students up to the chair to share a story, I am very comfortable adapting Horn and Giacobbe's language and process into my own teaching.

The students usually tell their stories in broken phrases and rambling sentences. I remind myself that the product (a perfectly crafted story with a logical sequence) is NOT my focus—yet. My purpose at this stage is to deepen our understanding that we write to communicate a message; therefore, we need to think carefully about our intended message (story), be clear, and

speak confidently. At the beginning of the year, sitting and speaking from
the storytelling chair can be a delightful experience for some children but a
frightening one for others. Because I have been carefully observing my students
for several weeks, I know who is ready to sit in the chair and who needs more
time to watch their peers tell stories.

I sit on the floor next to the student as she takes her place at the front of
the group. I remind the class of our purpose: "Jennifer is sharing a story with
us, and we will learn something new about her if we listen closely. We will
have time to ask her questions when she is finished, but just like when we are
solving a problem, this is Jennifer's time to speak first. Are we ready to listen to
Jennifer's story?"

This introduction establishes not only the expected behavior for listening
but also the *purpose* of listening. As Jennifer shares her story, I listen and nod
my head. I make surprised faces, and I repeat her story back to her when she
stalls. The tone of my voice and my animated body language can make even the
dullest trip to the grocery store sound thrilling.

Just as I did when I was the main storyteller, I have the students retell their
stories two or three times, letting them change and add or remove any parts. This
is not a lesson on the ability to retell a story; it is a lesson on communicating a
story orally. Adding characters, dropping a scene, or introducing a new problem
are accepted and encouraged because these same literacy lessons—revising,
adding dialogue, making inferences, and so on—will be covered throughout the
year. We also work on using full sentences, speaking clearly and fluently in our
oral storytelling.

This extended focus on oral storytelling can make some teachers panic.
Because there are so many items to cover in the writing curriculum, I also used
to believe that I had to dive into writing as soon as possible to give my students
enough time to learn the alphabet, handwriting skills, capitals and punctuation,
and many other components of writing. Over the years, however, I learned that
slowing down at the beginning can actually speed up the process at the end.
Think of it this way: we know from research that introducing subject content
and literacy skills to English language learners in their native language can help
them make connections to those same concepts when hearing them in English
(August 2006). My own experience with immigrant students bears this out. So
it seemed logical to apply the same principles to oral storytelling. Allowing
revising and editing lessons to flow without interruption in oral storytelling

helps children transfer the learning into their written work when those lessons are introduced later in the year.

A PICTURE TELLS A STORY

For our actual writing time, our focus is on illustrations and how they can help the reader understand the story. I share a short story of my own and model how to illustrate it. As I draw, I think out loud and retell my story again. I have a favorite story about the year my son, Griffin, started first grade. I use it every year, although he is now twenty-one! The story begins with us at the shoe store. Griffin couldn't decide on the best color. He tried on seven pairs of shoes, and each time I grew more and more impatient. When I reenact this with my students, I toss my arms out in pretend frustration and say, "Griffin, pick a pair of shoes!" in a singsong voice. By the third time, the students are acting it out and repeating the phrase with me.

"When Griffin and I walked into the store, I couldn't believe how many shoes there were! There were high tops and low tops, basketball shoes and soccer cleats, and shoes that had lights and shoes that made noises! I want the reader to see how many shoes there were, so I'm going to draw lots and lots of shelves," I tell my students.

Using an 18-by-24-inch piece of notebook paper for my story, I decide to take up the entire page for my drawing. This makes it easy for the children to see the details I will be adding as I retell my story.

"Now, there are the shoes and I need to put Griffin in here somewhere. Where should I put him?"

As a group, we discuss whether to have Griffin sitting or standing, where the shoe salesman should be, and where I will be standing. This conversation reinforces to the students that my drawing is my message; it needs to have good details in order to tell my story. After listening to their suggestions, I say, "Thanks for your ideas. I am the author and it is my story so I will decide what to draw. I'm going to put Griffin standing over here next to the mirror."

I continue retelling the story from the beginning before adding a new detail. I will not put any letters or words on my page yet. As we become proficient at telling and listening to stories, I begin to teach illustrating skills. I teach how to draw the setting to add depth to the moment. I teach the difference between coloring in and scribbling. I teach how to show movement with short lines after a running character, and how to draw people using shapes not lines. These artistic skills help develop the components of a strong story without the added anxiety of how to spell the word *sister*, or how to form a lowercase *g*, or how to hear the first sound in *cat*.

Having said this, I don't mean to imply that I forbid students from writing words or letters. Every classroom has a range of abilities, and differentiating for them is our daily challenge as primary grades teachers. Rather, my point is that by deemphasizing the focus on the written aspect of the story, I can individually support students—where they are—in the writing process. I will have Emma Ly label her characters because she can spell her mom and sister's names. Later, I will use her story to teach how to label. I will have Flori sound out the word *party* because she has attended preschool for two years and I know she has the sounds /p/, /r/, and /t/. When other students are ready, I will use her writing to teach them how to hear sounds too. As a group, we work on letters and sounds during other parts of the day.

After I have modeled how to draw a story, I call up other students to tell their stories and we discuss how they might add illustrations. I don't actually have them draw in front of the class as I did. Instead, we use our hands to show where they might put the house or how big they might draw Dad. If there is something that seems tricky, I might draw it on the whiteboard as an example but promptly erase it so it does not become a copying activity. After a few students have shared, we turn to a partner and ask, "What are you going to write about today?" During these short, two-minute conversations, I circulate to hear the students' writing plans. I want to hear that everyone has a story to start working on, and then we head off to our tables.

We spend several days drawing stories. Some students draw two or three a day; some work on the same story for two days in a row. We are developing our understanding of why we write and we are also developing our stamina. The familiar whine "I'm done!" is quickly squashed when we say, "Then start another one!" Again, working individually with students at this time allows me to stretch each one to his highest level. The children who can go back and see that they need to add more detail after a short conference will do so. Those who are still immature in their focus and language or motor skills will retell their story to me, add a detail with me, and then start drawing a new story. Forcing a student to work on one story would be counterproductive to my goal of making Writing Workshop the best part of the day!

REVIEWING READ-ALOUDS

After a week or so of illustrating stories, we begin to look at the covers of our favorite read-aloud books. We notice the shapes and colors and the size of the drawings and text. We wonder why the author chose the title and how the cover illustration makes us interested in reading the book. We spend several days creating our own covers using bold markers and bright backgrounds. (I tell the children there can be no white color showing on their cover drawing to ensure they are taking their time to create their cover.) We publish our wordless picture books by laminating the final cover to their story and stapling them together. We share these books with other classes and adults. With each reading our telling becomes stronger, more detailed, and we are forced to answer authentic questions from authentic readers—we are authors!

During Reading Workshop our retelling and fluency become more practiced as we extend our thinking to the main idea and the logical sequence of stories. We discuss how the stories we have read are similar to or different from the stories we tell and write. I take a great number of photographs during the day as the children are working and playing, and then I use these snapshots when making personalized books that stay in the children's book boxes for independent reading times. I use a free software program called RealeWriter by Unite for Literacy (www.realewriter.com). It is an incredibly easy-to-use self-publishing program that provides the formatting and layouts for printing guided reading books. The children love seeing their faces and names in real books! Some books have no words so the students can continue their work on developing strong story lines. Some books have one word on a page, naming the character or item. Some books have full sentences from page to page. I have found that the extra time it takes to create these individual books is worth it because teaching from what the children can already do—as Marie Clay (1988) says, "the known"—helps them develop the concentration and confidence that good readers need.

CIRCLING BACK TO THE CALM

Kindness and peacefulness are my favorite Friendship Workshop skills to introduce to students. I find it easy to incorporate these concepts into the entire curriculum because the representations are everywhere. The first year I taught a multiage classroom, my coteacher, Christy, and I laid out the requirements for the grades side by side and saw many skills that overlapped and would be easily accessible for the students (number sense in math, life cycles in science, and so on). However, the social studies curriculum always seemed a little dry to us, and we wondered how to make it more relevant for the children.

As we looked over the social studies standards, we saw that the program for both grades included citizenship skills, famous people, and an understanding of the passing of time, among other things. We planned a yearlong theme—Peacefulness: Then and Now. Our first action was to hang a string across the classroom as a time line with the title "We Are Peacemakers" (see Figure 8.4). The first pictures were of the students under a card that said, "2003. We use kind words to bring peace to our school." As the year progressed we added famous events and people (such as Martin Luther King Jr., Eleanor Roosevelt, Abraham Lincoln, George Washington Carver, and Betsy Ross) who also brought peace to the world, and each card contained the date and a short description of the peaceful act. The students enjoyed adding new people every few weeks.

When Christy and I realized that most of these people were dead (and, for the most part, white, which did not reflect our student population at all), we decided to include some (then) living peacemakers: the Dalai Lama, a Tibetan

Figure 8.4
Our peacemaker time line helps students connect historical people and deeds from the past to our choices and actions of today.

monk; Wangari Maathai, a Kenyan environmentalist; Cesar Chavez, a Mexican-American labor rights leader; Shirin Ebadi, an Iranian lawyer and human rights activist; Mother Teresa, an Albanian missionary; and others. We chose people of different nationalities who championed different causes to show the students that peacefulness starts from the desire of one person to make the world a better place. Each new person provided us with the opportunity to use picture books, videos, speeches, and the Internet to learn about these people and discuss their peacefulness. The last pictures that we hung on our time line that spring were new photos of the students under a card that said "2023" (the year they would graduate college). Each student wrote a sentence describing his or her hopes and dreams and how he or she would bring peace into the world.

Chapter 9

RESPONSIBILITY

Charlie was a bright, energetic first grader who had seen physical violence in his family. He shouted out in class, disrupted learning with his antics, physically annoyed his classmates, and threw materials when he became angry. He needed a great deal of extra attention to get through the day and he rarely took responsibility for his actions. Charlie's outbursts created an uneasy atmosphere in our classroom and I was unsuccessful in managing his needs and flare-ups.

Reflecting on Charlie's behavior, I saw that he was a quick learner, athletically strong, and street savvy, so most things came easily to him. However, when something proved difficult for Charlie, he got overwhelmed and irritated. For example, one afternoon during Science Workshop, Charlie's peers were able to make spinning tops, but for Charlie, confusion, self-doubt, and prideful machismo (all things I had been trying to address individually with him) set off an angry explosion. I suddenly saw Charlie's behavior in a new light and realized that he had no capacity to control his frustrations.

The next week, I taught the whole class the vocabulary word *frustration*. We made charts about things that frustrate us, drew pictures of what it looks and feels like to be frustrated, and brainstormed ways to deal with frustration. I made it clear that although this was Charlie's issue (they all knew it because they had experienced his outbursts), we all have frustrations in our lives and we can help each other deal with these difficult emotions.

Learning simple expressions such as "I am really angry right now!" or "That makes me very frustrated" helped most of the students cope, but Charlie needed more strategies. We created a chart like those hospitals use to indicate a patient's pain level. Low-end frustration was represented by a straight face, medium level was a furrowed brow and tight lips, and top of the chart was a funny sketch of a volcano erupting from the top of a head. Charlie used the chart when he was frustrated and circled the level he was feeling. He then used the words written underneath to describe his frustration, such as "I am feeling level-five frustrated and I need to take a break." Although the strategy of using the chart in these ways did not solve Charlie's anger issues, it gave him a new way to take responsibility for his behavior when he felt out of control.

Responsibility typically means being accountable for something, but it can also mean the ability to independently make decisions. Responsibility in a classroom incorporates both aspects. Students must be responsible for tangible things such as taking care of their materials and completing their homework, as well as for emotional responses such as moderating their behavior in class and with their peers. Charlie needed specific and individual support to become more responsible for his actions. The chart taught Charlie a specific strategy, and showed the other students that our choices affect everyone, and demonstrated to everyone that as a family of learners we are all responsible for creating a safe, respectful, and rigorous learning environment.

RESPECTED AND RECONNECTED

In Friendship Workshop our lessons about responsibility revolve around being honest and making good choices. We learn that when we make a mistake, we can feel safe admitting it and try to fix the problem when we can. For example, when my kindergarten students are playing in the block area and building towers, they learn to say, "If you didn't make it then you can't break it." However, if someone breaks a tower (which inevitably happens), they can say, "I'm sorry. Can I help you fix it?" It's important for the children to understand that when we make a mistake, the peacefulness and trust that we have strived to build in our community can feel broken. Sometimes it takes more than "I'm sorry" to repair those bonds. Responsive Classroom suggests teaching students how to make an apology of action that helps both parties feel respected and reconnected (Denton and Kriete 2000).

An apology of action "restores trust and a sense of harmony" (Fillion et al. 2005). It requires that the perpetrator find a way to realistically and respectfully make amends by choosing an action that is relevant to the situation. I have found that this system of apologizing helps diminish those lingering resentments that young children can carry with them after being hurt by a friend. The actions are usually simple and yet, quite genuine: a drawing of things they like about the person they hurt or choosing the student first at recess if they left him out the day before. Taking the apology beyond words reinforces our goal of talking about what hurts us in order to make our classroom a safe and fun place to be.

During Friendship Workshop, we also discuss how we can take responsibility for our learning by ignoring distractions. We might move if someone is bothering us or say, "Please stop. I am working now." We also practice self-talk to help us make good choices and try to be helpful to one another. When I know I will be out of the classroom for a day, I spend time discussing ways the students can help the substitute teacher. Most years I have only needed to remind the children about good behavior, but the year I taught Charlie, I knew the class would need very concrete responsibilities.

We made a T-chart with everyone's name and I asked, "How will you be responsible tomorrow and help the classroom run smoothly?" Next to each student's name, I wrote the suggested actions, such as "Showing the sub where the writing papers are" and "Helping the sub take attendance." The substitute teacher kindly put smiley faces next to the names of students who did their jobs as promised, and that was a big hit.

LEARNING THE RULES OF ENGAGEMENT

Conversation—an informal exchange of thoughts, ideas, and information—is an important component of literacy. As we bring more structure to the way we share and respond, particularly in academic settings, we move conversation toward discussion. In discussions, people generally share points of view and agree or disagree with the topic. Conversations and discussions also occur in literature, such as when two characters in a play or novel use talk to solve a problem, and then we have a dialogue. In each type of exchange, the participants have different roles to play, yet I'm struck by how often teachers forget to explain these parameters to students, to teach them about academic talk. Author and educator Maria Nichols (2006) calls classroom discourse "purposeful talk," because it requires taking turns in a conversation, holding a thought in our heads, integrating previous knowledge with new information, and a host of other skills.

Purposeful talk, Nichols writes in *Comprehension Through Conversation: The Power of Purposeful Talk in the Reading Workshop*, "is not something children do for a specified period of time during the day, but a way of being present and focused in a learning environment, a way of living as a learner" (2006, 8). In essence it is how students learn to take responsibility for their learning.

Young students have conversations all day long, but that does not mean they understand the rules of engagement. Because they are developmentally egotistical, children typically think only about their personal contributions to the conversation. They might shout out answers or thoughts when others are talking, without regard for what has actually been said. The skills of listening deeply and staying focused on a topic directly relate to self-control, and Friendship Workshop can be an easy way to introduce these qualities to the class.

I remember during Writing Workshop one day when I wanted to use Jessica's story to talk about how to create a logical flow and sequence events in a narrative. However, in one of those moments when the formal curriculum and the needs of my students collided, I chose a detour to intersperse lessons about listening and self-control along with the literacy plan.

Jessica had written a three-page story about her broken arm. It was sparse and lacked some critical details: "I went to the park. I fell off the swing. I couldn't swim." I wanted the students to listen carefully as Jessica read her story aloud and uncover the missing information (that Jessica had broken her arm and had to get a cast, which made swimming impossible). Yet, as soon as Jessica started sharing her story about going to the park, various students called out, "I've been there!" "They have tire swings there!" and "They're really cool." Jessica's share time turned into a chaotic din of whole-group jabbering.

The noise volume increased, and I realized that the children were only listening to the surface of the story. They did not understand the deeper purpose of listening thoughtfully to the writer's words. So I used our previously learned social skills of kindness and peacefulness to introduce the need for self-control. I reflected purposeful talk.

"Friends," I began, "it sounds like many of you have been to the same place Jessica has been. And it is exciting to share that with her, but I'm not feeling very peaceful right now. My ears hurt a little because we're so loud and my head feels fuzzy because we're talking on top of one another. Does anyone else feel this way?"

Several students nodded their heads in agreement and Jesus said, "And my eyes are going back and forth 'cause I don't know who to look at!"

"I agree, Jesus," I said. "It makes it hard to feel connected when so many things are happening at once. This is Jessica's time to share. We need to be responsible for our thoughts and voices. How can we do that?"

RESPECTFUL AND PRODUCTIVE CONVERSATIONS

There were suggestions of taking turns, raising hands, the typical answers students think a teacher wants to hear. And they were right—those actions would help—but it was imperative that I underline the reasons why the students would want to be responsible listeners. Not to make me happy, but to make our discussions and workshops more respectful and productive.

"So why would it feel better to take turns?" I asked the group. "Turn to the person next to you and discuss this."

I wandered from pair to pair, listening to their insights:

- "Because we could hear each other."

- "It means everyone would get a chance. That's fair."

- "Because what if you've never been to that park? Then you don't have anything to say when everyone else is talking."

The children certainly understood why they shouldn't interrupt. Now I had to think about how to help them practice and choose to listen before responding.

"I heard some great reasons and I want to share them with you so we all remember why we listen deeply when someone is talking. Here's what I heard . . ."

After sharing some of their reasons, I asked Jessica if it would be okay if she waited until tomorrow to finish reading her story. She agreed and sat back in her spot on the carpet. I then explained how I felt when I was talking and people interrupted me—like Jessica, I felt a little sad and ignored. I told of a time at the dinner table when I was young and no one had listened to my story. My eyes got hot and my mouth became dry from holding back tears. (I do not specifically recall this happening to me, but being the youngest of six, I am quite sure it did and I take poetic license in using it to illustrate the lesson.) I asked my students, did any of them ever feel this way? Every head nodded robustly; they had. "How about we use our writing time to draw and write about when this has happened to you?"

After working for about ten minutes we gathered back on the carpet to share our stories and drawings about being ignored by big brothers and sisters, of not being heard during conversations at Grandma's house when all the grown-ups were around, and other times when we had been left out of discussions. We shared how we felt (sad, lonely, mad) when someone interrupted or ignored us. We then talked about times when we were listened to, when someone paid close attention to our story and how that made us feel (happy, warm, cared for). Then we went off to draw a picture of those times. After another ten minutes we gathered once again and shared our work. We liked how we felt when someone paid attention to what we said, and we decided to learn how to listen to one another more carefully.

BECOMING BETTER LISTENERS

Over the next few weeks we got creative about identifying and being responsible for good listening habits. One suggested approach was creating a silent symbol, one hand placed on top of the other, to remind us not to talk on top of another person's comments. We tried to remember to listen for the silence before talking. We also learned phrases such as "Are you finished talking?" and "Can I add something?" before speaking. (Amusingly, the latter phrase did not always mean the next statement was actually connected to the speaker's topic, but it was a start!)

The initial Writing Workshop lesson that prompted our focus on being responsible listeners had not followed my plan to teach the logical sequence of stories. However, it had led us to the more important part of the literacy unit—listening. Rather than limiting our attention to the curricular objective of learning to listen to a specific story or person, we had learned how to listen well. In turn, our lessons about responsibility had opened the path to more valuable academic conversations down the road.

Figure 9.1 shows a graphic representation of the reflective process that I go through as I consider the possible causes of students' misbehaviors, observe their interpersonal relationships, and think of actions I could take to address their social and emotional needs in terms of responsibility and then to redirect their behavior. In the following section, I explore different sets of teacher reflections related to the Friendship Workshop topic of responsibility and discuss examples of how students' interactions might play out in the classroom.

DISORGANIZATION

Reflection Questions

Is the student a walking example of Pig-Pen from the Peanuts comic strip? Do you find her papers, materials, and miscellaneous clothing items strewn about the room on a daily basis? Is there anything she does organize well?

Possible Needs

I remember that when my son, Griffin, was young, it was sometimes easier for me to pick up his toys than to chase him down and make him do it. Most of the time, however, I held him responsible for taking care of his messes. Some students may not have much experience cleaning up their surroundings, putting away their playthings, or organizing their backpacks. Some students may not have much experience with ownership. They may have to share most things with their siblings, or perhaps they have so many material things that nothing feels precious to them. There is a sense of pride that comes from taking

Behaviors

Disorganized   Evading the truth

Physically agitated   Poor communication skills

Easily distracted

Looking "busy" but disconnected

Figure 9.1
Developing
Responsibility

Reflection Questions

When does it occur?   With whom?

What exactly is the student doing?

Is the student distracted by others (or causing the distraction)?

Does the student know how to hold a productive conversation?

Is the student always scrambling to find materials?

Are personal belongings scattered and messy?

Does the student verify what the rules (and
consequences) are?

Possible Needs

Sense of pride

Learn the give and take of conversing

Clarification of good and poor choices

Protect ego (not make a mistake)

Learn how to apologize

care of something that is "just mine," and some students may need to build an understanding of that pride through small, concrete tasks.

Possible Actions

Choose one or two tasks that you want the students to be responsible for handling. A simple chart posted in their cubbies or at their desks can serve as a reminder. For example, (1) Turn in homework and (2) Tie shoes. A high five when tasks are completed can start the child off with a positive attitude for being responsible.

One year, my colleague Melissa Fleischer had a fifth grader who struggled with responsibility. Melissa laminated a library envelope and taped it to Naomi's desk. Then she and Naomi sat down and discussed the things Naomi had to be responsible for throughout the day. They chose a dozen tasks such as completing her reader response journal, returning her library book, and having three sharpened pencils at her desk. Melissa typed up the tasks on individual cards and Naomi drew pictures to accompany them. All twelve cards were placed in the library envelope.

Whenever Naomi completed a task, she would pull the card out of the envelope and give it to Melissa. At the end of the day, the two would tally up the number of tasks Naomi had responsibly handled, and at the end of the week she received a small reward, depending on how many tally marks she had earned. Using the same cards over and over reinforced to Naomi that responsibility is a daily duty and that being responsible meant she had choices to make throughout the day.

Another teacher I know set up a routine for a student who struggled with being prepared to work. She set aside a few minutes at the end of the day for the boy to put up the new schedule cards for the following day. They briefly discussed what materials he would need and what choices he would need to make (colored pencils for writing workshop, which reading center to work in, and so on). By January, the student could change the cards and prepare his desk independently.

APOLOGIZING

Reflection Questions

Do students balk when having to take responsibility? Do they deny or deflect their responsibilities? Can they apologize sincerely when necessary?

Possible Needs

Trusting that someone will still like you after making a mistake is easier said than believed. Toddlers believe that if they cover their eyes so they cannot see you, then it must hold true that you cannot see them either. Young students may have similar beliefs—if they don't admit to a mistake then maybe it never really happened. They need to feel certain they will be accepted even after a mistake.

Possible Actions

Sometimes my students need a few days or a more intimate setting to be able to apologize. I allow this if the perpetrator is repeatedly making the same small mistake or when the mistake is not serious in nature, such as nudging in line or not making room on the carpet for a friend. Having a Lunch Bunch session can provide a safer environment for the involved parties to come together and discuss the situation. In some cases, students may lack the vocabulary to express regret. "I" statements empower students to be mindful of what happened and what they can do to fix the problem. Rather than saying, "You wrote on my paper!" a student may say, "I did not like it when you wrote on my paper." This clearly identifies the problem while reducing any argumentative feelings. This can help the other student feel more at ease when apologizing.

CONVERSATIONAL SKILLS

Reflection Questions

Do certain students seem disconnected from peer-to-peer conversations? Do they blank out or ramble on about an unrelated topic? Can they have a back-and-forth dialogue on a topic of interest, or is the talk usually one-sided?

Possible Needs

Having a successful conversation requires very sophisticated communication skills, including the ability to negotiate meaning, clarify misunderstandings, exchange ideas, and synthesize new information. For young students, learning each of those skills requires patient instruction and hours of practice. If many of my students have not come from language-rich backgrounds, I may need to break down the give-and-take of conversation for them.

For example, I may pair Jessica and Rabia together if Rabia is struggling with negotiating meaning during buddy reading. I would be Rabia's "voice" to model how to ask a question that helps my understanding. I would say, "I am going to ask Jessica to help me understand." The following day I would do the same thing but ask Rabia to ask my question. The following day I would help Rabia form a question. Each day I would model a conversation skill and slowly release the responsibility to Rabia. *Comprehension Through Conversation* (2006) and *Talking About Text* (2008) by Maria Nichols are fabulous books that explain how to do this type of conversation work in whole-group discussions.

Possible Actions

In her books, Nichols offers many powerful ways to teach students how to have purposeful and productive conversations. "Listening with Intent," for example, requires pausing long enough to be sure someone has fully finished his or her thought before we respond or comment. "Keeping the Lines of Thinking Alive" piggybacks on that by teaching students to sustain a train of thought. They learn to think critically and use the information to form or support their own opinions on a particular topic.

MAKING GOOD CHOICES

Reflection Questions

Are certain students easily distracted by others? Are they nosy, interfering in others' business throughout the day? Can they allow different rules for different students or do they become a "rule enforcer," reporting all misdeeds of their classmates?

Possible Needs

Learning to make good choices is a lifelong skill. We all struggle at times when we are torn between two (or more) options. As an adult, I'm still learning how to make good choices, so I can't expect my young students to have mastered the process by the age of seven! When I think about how to break down the skill for young learners, I realize that one of the tricky parts is recognizing that we always have options. Children often get stuck when asked to think abstractly. They are concrete and reactionary learners, focused on the immediate and the obvious, so they need help considering possibilities.

Possible Actions

"Rule enforcers" are hypervigilant about other people following the rules. They may be chronic rule breakers themselves but they refuse to allow anyone to break a rule without receiving punishment. This is where the definition between punishment and consequence needs to be clearly defined for students. I discuss with my students that we establish rules to set a foundation of appropriate behavior for our community, but we must also be flexible with those rules because sometimes there are extenuating circumstances. This directly connects to our empathy lessons. When a peer is having a difficult day and we allow him to sit in the rocking chair (even though it's not his designated day), we create a safe space for that student to gain control. Highlighting such examples when they occur naturally in the school day can help students see how we use our rules as a starting point and we then make choices based on individual needs.

I use choice cards (index cards or laminated sheets of paper) to provide simple solutions to some of the common problems in classroom communities. On one side, I place words and illustrations of the problems, and on the other side I list possible actions: Move your seat, Take a break, Ask a friend, Tell a grown-up. I created the choice cards one year because of Ali, who joined our kindergarten class in mid-December from Iraq. Ali had not been to school before because, his mother explained, it was too dangerous for them to leave the house. I remember when Mrs. Sisk, our school secretary, brought Ali to our classroom.

"Ms. Buckley, you have a new student joining your class this morning," she said.

I know families move to be safer, I know parents get new jobs and relocate, and I know children rarely enjoy coming to a new school midyear, but still I flinched when I saw Ali coming. New students enrolling late in the school year have missed so much: not just curriculum, although that is true, but also the class-building activities, the trust games we have played, and the community rules we have agreed to support that have helped establish our well-functioning classroom. At this point in the term, our rules and routines had become second nature and students had become much more independent. Selfishly, I worried that trying to fast-forward a new student would disturb our sense of order.

"He moved here last week from Iraq and he doesn't know much English yet," continued the school secretary. "This is his mom, and I will take her to the cafeteria to set up his account now." Ali's mom smiled gloriously, took my hands in hers, and bowed her head several times. "Thank you, thank you for taking care of my son. Thank you very much," she said before hurrying off. I noticed that Ali's big brown eyes were close to tears when I walked him toward an empty cubby to hang up his coat and backpack. Then I led him to an empty seat and introduced him to Adolfo.

"Adolfo, this is our new friend, Ali," I said. "Can you show him what you are drawing?"

Adolfo quietly slid his paper toward Ali and explained that he was drawing the lake he goes to with his dad. I gave Ali a blank paper and some crayons and mimed a drawing. There were other parents dropping off book fair money and permission slips so I left Ali and Adolfo alone but kept my eye on that corner. Ali silently and a little tearfully sat staring at the door.

His silent pattern continued for several days. He came to the door in the morning and waited for me to lead him to his cubby. I helped him hang up his backpack and coat and led him to his table. Adolfo showed Ali what to do for morning work and Ali sat and watched. All day he quietly followed the class from activity to activity. On the playground he ran and swung by himself and I thought I saw him talking to himself but with others he remained silent.

MORE THAN WORDS CAN SAY

Ten minutes after the students left for the cafeteria on Friday, a teacher brought Ali back into the classroom for biting another student. This seemed so out of character for the passive boy I knew thus far. Ali couldn't explain himself and when I mimicked the act of biting someone he remained frozen. A phone call to his mom revealed that he had never done this before; she was so embarrassed. I reassured her that it was most likely a phase and together we would help Ali make better choices. Ali gave his mom no specific reason for his behavior and she promised to speak with him when he got home from school.

Ali came in the next morning with his mother and shyly said, "I sorry." I hugged him and told him it was good to apologize. We walked over to his cubby and hung up his backpack, and he joined his classmates at the table. He took out paper and crayons and began drawing a scene similar to Adolfo's lake picture from earlier in the week.

Slowly Ali became more vocal and said good morning to his classmates when it was his turn. He would rush up to the book I was reading, point to the illustrations, and ask, "What that?" He was trying out new English words, learning where the drawing materials were kept, and recognizing dismissal time. On the playground, I watched as he joined the game of tag with his classmates. He ran and shouted and laughed. He even chased Adolfo when Adolfo wasn't playing!

Lunchtime came and Ali was back in the classroom for biting a student again. What was going on? What was bothering him? Another talk with mom, another set of apologies, another promise of no more. The cafeteria assistant saw nothing that provoked Ali and reported that the students were all pleasant to Ali at the table.

I had no Arabic words in my bag of tricks but luckily we had an Arabic-speaking parent liaison who could help me with some basic directions: please walk, sit down, no biting. I realized I would also have to use pictures and symbols to really help Ali. I created some cards that depicted simple requests. One card had a hand saying, "Stop, please," and another had a picture of our peace table and said, "Take a break." Another showed a picture of three seats with an X through the middle one. It said, "Space, please." I had the liaison help me explain these terms to Ali and he used them to let us know what he needed.

Later I used the cards during a Friendship Workshop focusing on choices. We pretended Jeffrey was being bothered by Samuel during writing. I explained to the class, "Jeffrey has a decision to make. He has two choices. He can talk with Samuel and not get his writing done or he can ask for 'Space, please.'" We showed the two cards (the other had a simple stick figure with a big speech bubble filled in with "blah, blah, blah") and discussed which was a good choice. Another time we pretended Sofia was bothered by Raneem during Morning Meeting. Raneem kept trying to whisper in Sofia's ear and when Sofia asked for space Raneem ignored her. The class brainstormed ideas and decided that moving to a new seat would be a good choice. We drew up the choice cards: one that showed a stick figure whispering to another figure and one that showed the stick figure walking away. Several lessons like this helped the students understand that they had options when confronted with sticky situations. They would name the choices and choose the best one.

As for Ali, the next day I stood at the back of the cafeteria and watched him during lunch. I realized Ali was biting the same student every time—Adolfo— and I wondered why. Ali copied all the drawings Adolfo did in the mornings, he always chose the same math center as Adolfo, and he chased Adolfo at recess. Maybe Ali wanted to sit with his friend but didn't have the words to say so. In addition to not knowing how to ask permission to join Adolfo in English, Ali also seemed not to understand the cultural process of being socially engaged. I watched as Ali glanced at the assistant, who was opening milk for someone. Slowly he got up from his seat and walked over to Adolfo's table. As much as I was fascinated by Ali's problem-solving choice, I couldn't let him bite Adolfo again, so I stepped in. I said, "Ali, do you want to sit here?" as I pointed to Adolfo's table. Ali's eyes grew extra-large and he nodded his head enthusiastically. "Let's ask Adolfo then. You say, 'Adolfo, can I sit here?'" Ali quietly mumbled the question to Adolfo and Adolfo said, "Yes." We made room for Ali and his lunch tray. Ali did not engage with Adolfo or the others at the table but his face had softened and he smiled for the rest of the day. I went back to the room and made a card for Ali that had a picture of two stick figures arm in arm. It said, "Friend, please." (See Ali and Adolfo reading together in Figure 9.2.)

RESPONSIBILITY IN ACTION

Responsibility for learning is a crucial skill for students' success. At this young age remembering to hand in a note from home, where to put the homework folder, or to wear sneakers on P.E. days are the beginning steps of being responsible. Learning to be responsible for our thoughts and actions introduces students to the internal sense of pride that comes from learning.

I remember working with a small math group in my multiage K–1 class. Rojo, a kindergartner, had explained his math thinking to me but Sammy, a first grader, was still confused. I watched as Rojo reread the math question one item at a time, making Sammy act out each step with manipulatives. Rojo changed his language from explaining (to me, an adult who knew the answer) to teaching (to Sammy, a peer who was confused). I saw in that exchange that Rojo had taken full responsibility for his own learning as well as Sammy's. The next chapter describes ways to instill this sense of pride and responsibility during our Writing and Reading Workshop.

Figure 9.2
Ali and Adolfo take turns reading a book.

Chapter 10

SELF-CONTROL

Self-control is probably the one skill teachers hope students will have in place before entering their classrooms. Self-control means students share materials respectfully, move thoughtfully and smoothly through learning centers, and minimize interruptions during guided reading groups. In short, the classroom runs itself. Self-control also includes modulating voices, restraining excessive body movements, organizing time and materials—the list goes on and on. During conversations (especially academic conversations), self-control requires the ability to manage internal thoughts, recognize confusions or misunderstandings, ask for clarification, and synthesize information.

Sometimes a student's lack of self-control is actually her attempt to create a sense of control. She may feel inadequate in a situation, and immaturity causes her to act impulsively. She may shout out, get physical with others, misuse materials, or become defiant. Trying to deal with these behaviors before I formally implemented Friendship Workshop lessons often frustrated me. How many times could I repeat "I understand you are excited to share your thinking, but right now it is Angel's turn to talk. Show respectful listening" without driving myself bonkers? My patience typically wore thin when students could not demonstrate self-control. I realized that explicit and regular instruction of the skills that lead to self-control had to become part of the curriculum in my classroom.

IN CHARGE OF OUR EMOTIONS

Because of our earlier Friendship Workshop lessons during the semester, students have by now learned what it means to be peaceful and what our faces and bodies feel like when we are content. They can recognize and name their emotions. They are conscious of kind words and use them more often. Next we move to self-control, including noticing when our bodies feel different and taking steps to calm down *before* we act.

Watching the children at recess I easily find events to illustrate the need for self-control.

"Did too!"

"Did not!"

"I tagged you! You're it now!"

"Am not!"

Everett lunges at Marcos and swings his fist to hit him but misses. He kicks the mulch angrily and continues to shout at Marcos.

I step in and say to the boys, "I can see Everett's body is tense and his voice is loud. He sounds angry. I saw part of what happened. Everett, can you tell me what happened from the beginning?"

Everett shouts, "It's all Marcos's fault! He always says he gets me but he doesn't touch me!"

I place my hand on Everett's shoulder and ask him to slow down. "Look at me, Everett." He glances up at my face. "I'm right here and I want to listen but I can't understand you if you shout. Can you take three deep breaths with me?" Everett and I take the deep breaths and I can see his shoulders drop just a little and his feet stop kicking the mulch.

"Now I see you're a little more relaxed. Do you want to tell me what happened?"

Everett takes another breath and begins again. "We were playing tag and Marcos was it. He chases everybody and when he gets tired he chases me and says he tagged me but he didn't touch me. He didn't."

Marcos put his hands on his hips and starts to interrupt but I stop him. "Marcos, it is Everett's turn to talk. He will explain what happened and how he is feeling and then you will get a turn. That way we can all listen to each other and understand how to fix it. Okay?"

Marcos sighs heavily but agrees and puts his arms down.

Everett continues, "He didn't tag me."

I repeat exactly what Everett has shared and ask if my summary is correct. He says yes, and now it is Marcos's turn to explain. However, I want to guide this discussion a little bit because I saw the incident and, in all honesty, Marcos did not actually touch Everett.

"Marcos, Everett says when you were playing tag you said you tagged him but he didn't feel it. Are you sure you tagged Everett?"

"I was running really fast and Everett always says he's not it but I reached out and tagged him in the back," Marcos says. His words are rapid and angry.

"I can tell you are frustrated because you are talking so fast," I respond. "Your voice sounds really angry. Can you take a breath with me?" Marcos and I take a breath and I continue, "I did see you running. Both of you were very fast. I'm wondering if you two were going so fast that maybe you reached out to tag Everett but you just got his jacket. Do you remember feeling Everett's back when you tagged him?"

Marcos pauses for a second and says he put his arm out and got Everett, maybe just lightly, but he did get him. We talk a little more and then I have the boys demonstrate the difference between a "heavy tag" and a "light tag." The other students who have been playing tag join us, and Everett and Marcos agree that maybe they are both right because there are different kinds of tags. They decide to come up with tag rules some other time and return to the swings for the rest of recess.

Later that day during Friendship Workshop we replay this situation because it was real. Everyone saw it happen, and it was a perfect example of how self-control helped fix the situation. I have Everett explain how he took three deep breaths and slowed down his frustration. I ask him if he felt better after taking the deep breaths and he tells the class, "Yeah. I was mad but then I felt quieter. We got to play for the rest of recess and that's good."

Self-control is an extension of feeling calm. Building on the calming-down lessons we learned earlier in the year, Everett is now able to be part of the solution and make a choice to play a different game rather than keep the argument going or stomp off in frustration. Self-control allows students to evaluate the pros and cons of a situation and make a deliberate choice—ideally a choice that helps them feel calm and peaceful.

MINDFULNESS

Friendship Workshop lessons about self-control focus on managing our physical bodies (hands, feet, and voices), but the real message is that we must pay attention to what's happening in our minds. If we monitor our internal thoughts and feelings, we learn to reflect before we act, and we wait patiently and interrupt politely—all components of self-control. Research indicates that teaching mindfulness has positive results on students' academic performance (Payton et al. 2008).

To reinforce the importance of mindfulness and self-control, we role-play different situations and come up with an anchor chart of ways to pass the time while waiting for our turn to talk. (Counting to one hundred is a popular way for kindergartners; skip-counting backward is a fun challenge for first and second graders.) The children discover that quietly humming a song to themselves, playing a hand-clapping game, or playing the I Spy game are among the ways we can train ourselves to wait patiently. Playing board games with the class or Hangman on the whiteboard are other fun ways to teach patience to a group of students. We also share ways that the children can wait patiently outside of school, such as when going to the doctor's office or the grocery store.

WAIT TIME AND PATIENCE

Have you ever been working with a student and felt the frantic rhythmic tapping of another child's finger on your shoulder? When this happens to me, I capture the culprit's finger under my palm, turn to him and say, "I don't hit you. You don't hit me. Wait patiently." Then when I am finished, I turn to the offending student and say, "Thank you for waiting patiently. When your body is in control it's easier to help you."

Every year as a class, we come up with a signal to let each other know when we need help or need to wait. Some years our signal was putting up one finger to indicate, "I will help you in one minute." Another year the class loved using sticky notes, so we made a "Help Center" where the children could find markers and sticky notes to write their names and the number one, two, or three to reflect the urgency of their needs. When they needed my help, the children would place the notes next to where I was working. It's true that almost everyone seemed to have a No. 1 problem that year, but the process did help students learn to pause before asking for help.

In addition to teaching young students how to wait patiently, we must give them permission to interrupt politely during acute moments. My main lesson focuses on using the words *Excuse me*, primarily

- when someone is in the way,

- when they need to ask a quick question, or

- in an emergency.

The first example I share is an extension of the kindness lessons. When walking past someone in a crowded lunch line, when reaching for a pencil that rolled under someone else's desk, or when finding a seat on the bus, we should say "Excuse me." Our gesture of thoughtfulness usually doesn't require an answer. Rather, the person might give a visual acknowledgment that she sees you are entering her space politely.

The second way we use the courtesy "Excuse me" is to signal respect for other people, such as when they are talking to someone else or focused on their work. When we do this, we let other people finish their actions or thoughts and then give us their full attention. For example: "Excuse me, Ms. Buckley. [Pause.] Can I take this to the library?" We also discuss how being in control when asking a question makes it easier for people to extend a helping hand because they are not abruptly interrupted.

The third way we use "Excuse me" is to seek help when we need immediate attention. Using the words *Excuse me* without the pause still indicates that you are in control but need help right away. For example: "Excuse me, Ms. Buckley, Sofia is throwing up in the math center" lets me know that the children are focused on the problem and want to help their friend. (Plus, it is a much nicer way to help than shouting, "Eww, gross! Sofia's puking!")

ANALYZING STUDENTS' BEHAVIORS

The Handbook of Personality and Self-Regulation, edited by Rick Hoyle, explains that the development of self-regulation skills is central to children's emerging sense of self as learners and can directly shape their belief in their abilities (2010). Preschool programs that offer high-quality programs focusing on self-regulatory skills have been shown to have a positive effect on academic achievement in later years as well as other positive long-term life outcomes such as home ownership, longer and more stable relationships, and less negative involvement with the law (Neuman and Dickinson 2011; Schweinhart et al. 2005; Hoyle 2010).

Self-regulation means a person is metacognitively, socially, motivationally, and behaviorally active in his or her own problem-solving processes. Students use self-awareness, self-talk, and self-evaluation to process information. They plan and manage their time effectively; absorb, combine, and categorize their experiences; and maintain a positive sense of self-esteem. Self-regulated learners create productive surroundings, expect learning to be a positive and rewarding experience, and can advocate for themselves (Kadhiravan and Suresh 2008).

Figure 10.1 shows a graphic representation of the reflective process that I go through as I consider the possible causes of students' misbehaviors, observe their interpersonal relationships, and think of actions I could take to address their social and emotional needs in terms of self-control and then to redirect their behavior. In the following section, I explore different sets of teacher reflections related to the Friendship Workshop topic of self-control and discuss examples of how students' interactions might play out in the classroom.

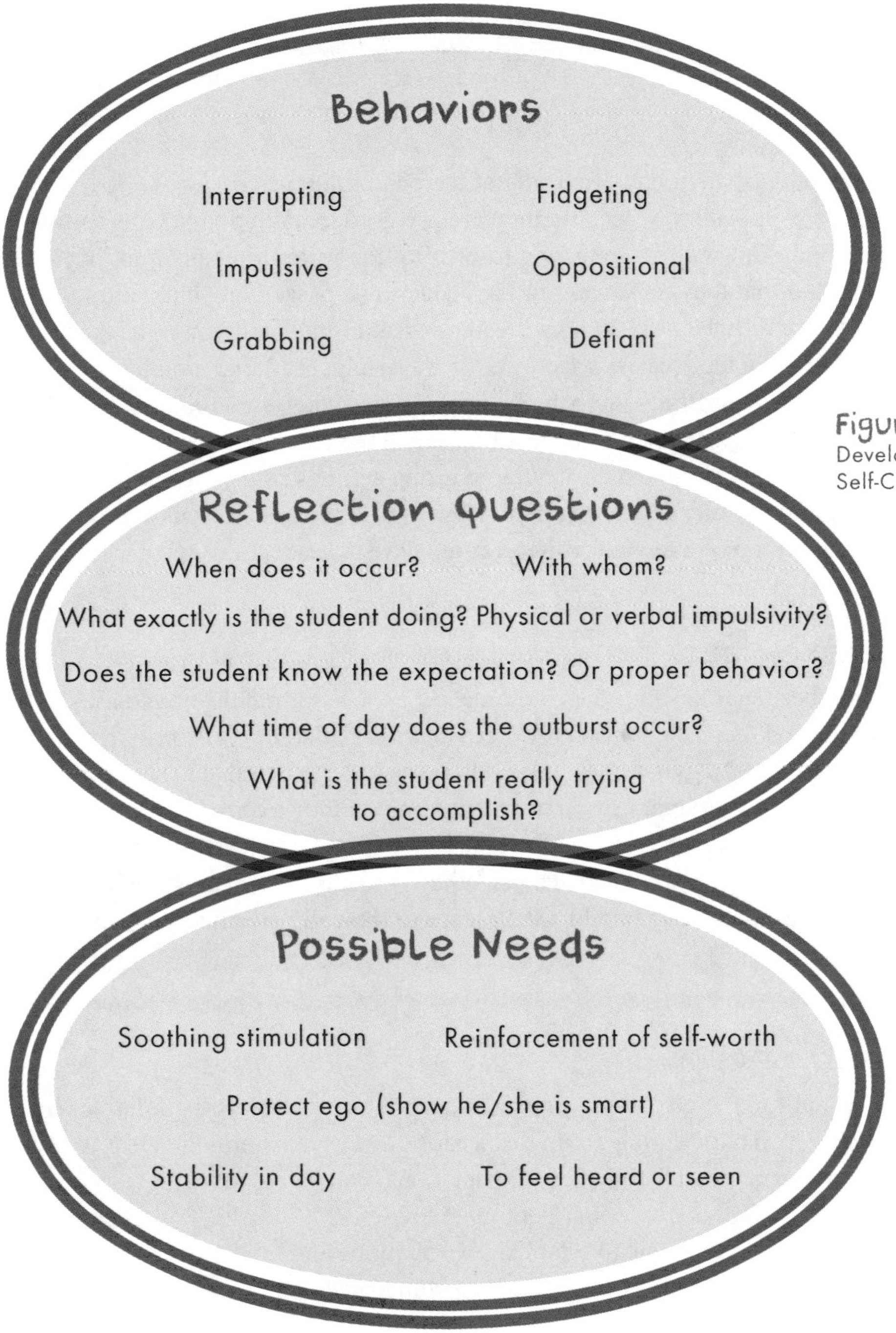

Behaviors

Interrupting   Fidgeting

Impulsive   Oppositional

Grabbing   Defiant

Figure 10.1
Developing
Self-Control

Reflection Questions

When does it occur?   With whom?

What exactly is the student doing? Physical or verbal impulsivity?

Does the student know the expectation? Or proper behavior?

What time of day does the outburst occur?

What is the student really trying
to accomplish?

Possible Needs

Soothing stimulation   Reinforcement of self-worth

Protect ego (show he/she is smart)

Stability in day   To feel heard or seen

INAPPROPRIATE INTERRUPTIONS

Reflection Questions

When students shout out, especially at the beginning of the school year, many times it is simply because they are not used to having to take turns for *everything*. They can grasp having to wait for the water fountain, and they understand that they must wait for the snack to be passed out, but waiting to talk? That's silly because I know the answer and I must tell you now!

I know the tendencies of five- and six-year-olds, so I explain how to behave in group settings and why waiting patiently helps our conversations flow respectfully. If some students don't grasp the message, I have to ask myself, Do they shout out only in large group settings or in all groups? Do their interruptions occur only during math lessons or during any discussion time? Do they talk on top of everyone or just certain classmates?

Possible Needs

I remember reading somewhere that a child's job is to find the boundaries of behavior and then try to push past them to see if the adult will consistently reinforce them. In gymnastics we often use a spotting belt that is rigged to the ceiling. It allows gymnasts to practice flipping on the balance beam without fear of falling. In the classroom, rules are like spotting belts in that they help students maintain emotional balance. When students push against the boundaries and their teachers offer stability, they learn to trust and eventually develop self-control.

Possible Actions

As the adult in the classroom, I need to establish clear and firm guidelines for children's behavior during group discussions. I must also provide clear ways for them to successfully meet my expectations. One of my favorite resources is *The First Six Weeks of School* (Denton and Kriete 2000), which outlines hour by hour and day by day how to establish expectations and guidelines for meeting them. The suggestions for organizing Morning Meeting and outdoor time are especially helpful. Day One consists of the teacher's introducing students, leading a simple song, and reading a short message. The rest of the week follows the same pattern, with the teacher gradually releasing control and allowing the students to introduce themselves, point out words on the song chart, and answer questions after reading the morning message. Meeting rules are created through discussion and reflection.

Recess is a valuable time, and *The First Six Weeks of School* explains how to use playtime to build friendships, learn procedures, and become familiar with the expectations of working in groups. The book's appendix lists games that ensure that all voices are heard and all students participate successfully.

It's important for teachers to be diligent during the first weeks of school to let students know where the boundaries are, help them understand that they must work within these boundaries, and consistently show them that respect flows in both directions. Some students may need to have a checklist of behaviors to remind them of the expectations. A list might have the heading "Am I . . ." and then include items such as "sitting with personal space," "raising my hand," and "asking, 'Are you finished?'" before speaking. Some years I have kept checklists at the front of the room so I could hand them to certain students when we gather in whole-group settings. Some of my colleagues ask particular students to keep a checklist in their pockets; a quick tap on the leg reminds the student of the expectations.

Most special education departments have the software Boardmaker (www.mayer-johnson.com) or similar programs for creating symbol-based cards to use with students. The illustrations depict most classroom activities and can be a quick and respectful way to help a student gain self-control.

BODY CONTROL

Reflection Questions

Does the student exhibit unusual physical movements, such as standing while writing, rocking back and forth while listening, or spinning while waiting in line? Does the student need extra physical movement throughout the day or just at certain times or during certain activities?

Possible Needs

Sensory integration is how the brain gathers and interprets incoming information through sight, sound, touch, and so on. Studies suggest strong links between the cerebellum (the part of the brain vital to motor control) and memory, attention, language, and decision making (Jensen 2005). Most young students develop sensory integration through typical childhood activities such as swinging, running, jumping, and rolling. Because so many schools are limiting recess and structured playtime and children spend more time in front of televisions and computers when at home, the opportunities to develop these vital neural connections, release stress, and refresh the attention are being lost.

Possible Actions

Make recess a priority! Kids need to play.

Check with the special education team for good ways to promote small-movement stimulation in the classroom. Ball chairs and balance chairs and other sensory objects can help. I have used extra-fuzzy carpet remnants for sitting and short-feathered boa yarn for holding (the stroking movement can be soothing) in whole-group learning situations.

Schedule consistent breaks in a student's personal schedule that allow for gross-motor movement. For example, taking a note to the office every morning after Math Workshop can help ease anxiety before it causes off-task behaviors.

INATTENTION

Reflection Questions

The infamous report card comment "Rachel has difficulty staying on task" covers everything—and nothing, really. What, specifically, does the student do when she is off task? Does she sit and talk loudly, or does she move aimlessly about the classroom? Does she disturb others, or does she become distracted by a book or an object? In what ways can she sustain focus?

Possible Needs

Children can go off task for many reasons. The two most common reasons I
have found are

1.   being unsure about or unconfident in their ability to complete the task and

2.   having a poor concept of time.

Possible Actions

If certain students are disturbing others, check that they know what is expected
of them during the activity. Perhaps they are unsure of the directions or feel
incapable of completing the task.

One of my students, Giselle, was a wanderer. Whenever Math Workshop
started she would leave the area and talk to her classmates, stand near the
manipulatives until she could decide whether to use the Unifix cubes or counting
bears, or stand quietly by me and wait. When I questioned her she would say
she needed my help to get started. Giselle knew what to do and how to do it but
wanted me next to her, reassuring her that she was doing it correctly.

After many discussions that produced no significant improvement in her
behavior, I was finally able to understand that Giselle felt intimated by math
in general (her number sense wasn't strong, but she was capable of doing the
work), so I assigned her a go-to buddy. Giselle would go to Jorelle three times
for questions or reassurance before she could wander or come to me. (I chose
Jorelle because he was a strong math student and he understood he was not to
tell Giselle the answer but help her feel confident about her work.)

Another way to be sure students understand the activity is to break it
down into very small chunks. Explain that they must complete each portion
and then have it checked by the teacher. This reassures students that they are
capable and lessens the sense of doom when looking at a full worksheet page of
multiplication problems.

For other students, tools to improve time management might be needed.
Managing time is hard enough for me as an adult. I may need to make copies,
find a book in the science lab, and check in with a colleague who isn't feeling
well—all in the ten minutes before kids arrive for the day. The pressure can
rattle me. Now imagine how it feels for young students when asked to juggle

tasks such as handing in their folders, getting their library books, and writing down tomorrow's homework before heading to music class. When their concept of time management is limited to waiting for their birthday party or Christmas to arrive, events that seem to take forever to finally happen, they may think they have all the time in the world to finish their art projects!

Young students may need very concrete ways to measure time. Consider bringing a windup egg timer to class. You can tell a student he needs to wait three minutes before getting a drink, for example. Always start small so the child feels immediate success, and then gradually increase the time. A laminated grid for the week upon which each task (for example, ten minutes reading independently) is checked off when completed successfully can help students see their progress and extend their focus.

Some students will need a more tangible reward for developing self-control. They may be struggling with connecting their effort (time) to the final product. Breaking down the lessons into small portions with short breaks in between (a drink at the water fountain or ten pushups) can help. Or, you might allot ten minutes for writing (break), ten minutes for illustrating (break), and ten minutes for writing. A simple check mark at each completed section provides a visual connection that students can use to track their progress.

Self-control also requires students to manage their impulses, internalize rules, and adjust to changing circumstances. These tasks, combined with the challenges of learning academic content and skills, can overwhelm some students. It is important to remember that improvements may take time, but students will gradually increase their ability to take deliberate action, plan ahead, and make mindful choices when we scaffold their learning into achievable steps.

LITERACY CONNECTIONS: RESPONSIBILITY AND SELF-CONTROL CONNECT TO READING AND WRITING FICTION AND DRAMATIZING MINI-PLAYS

One day after an author-sharing event in which my students presented their writing to another class, my friend and colleague Lauren Nye Schrum paid me a high compliment. "I thought my students were writing well but then I saw your kids," she told me. "They are so confident in speaking, clear in their reading, connected to their stories. How do you do it?"

Lauren is a strong teacher who always reflects on her practice to find new ways to reach students, so her praise moved me deeply. I mulled over her question for days. When I started to list the things I had done that year to see if any noticeable differences emerged, I was stumped. Like me, Lauren read great stories, used her Morning Message for word work, and incorporated hands-on learning for authentic writing lessons. So what had I done to get such good results with my students?

I thought about Adam, who had blossomed during the month of November. He went from usually writing simplistic events ("I go to the park") to working on the same complex story for more than a week. He told his story every day during Morning Meeting. It was about his family's being scared by a toy spider in the Halloween store. We all delighted at hearing how they shouted and hid and how Adam's little sister was the brave one who touched the spider first. Adam's typical string of letters developed into short chunks of letters, and his invented spellings for *spider* and *Halloween* became recognizable.

I thought of Flori, carefully placing a large gum eraser between each word of her story to mark where spaces needed to go in her "second edition." The office secretary loved Flori's book about getting dressed up for her six-year-old birthday party, and Flori wanted to give her a copy. Sharing her writing with others, a regular part of our Writing Workshop, had helped Flori become comfortable relating to an audience. Although she was usually cautious and soft-spoken, she became animated and bold when we went on a "book tour" to share our writing with different classrooms and adults within the school. She would strut right up to an adult and say, "I'm Flori, what's your name? Would you like to hear my story?" She was confident reading her story, answering questions, and giving details of her writing process.

And how could I forget Maria's mom coming to our Author Share with her one-week-old baby. She sat with every student, listening and smiling as they read their stories. The amazing part—Maria's mom didn't understand English. Yet she and the children felt the connection and the pride in being real authors, and her delight inspired them to work harder.

So what did I do that helped my students write so much and so well? It finally came down to the way I connected lessons to two critical elements: cultivating community and encouraging play. When we honestly delight in students' stories about their cut knees, their birthday piñatas, and their tickets won at Chuck E. Cheese's, we teach them that they have something important to say. And when they discover the power of sharing the events of their lives, in finding an audience for their work, they believe in their ability to write and communicate. Our time together in the classroom shows them they are interesting and interconnected. As they build the bonds of friendship, they learn to trust and respect each other. And when they FEEL that, they write more.

As for play, it is essential for young learners and a fundamental part of developing self-control. Children use dramatic play to try out new personality traits, sort out confusions, and organize their activities. The National Association for the Education of Young Children writes in "Developmentally Appropriate Practice and Play" that "Such play is influential in developing self-regulation, as children are highly motivated to stick to the roles and rules of the play, and thus grow in the ability to inhibit their impulses, act in coordination with others, and make plans" (National Association for the Education of Young Children 2009). Of course, the work of school is serious, but learning is also fun, and the goal of primary education should be to affirm that for children. If we guide the natural joy and exuberance of young students, we can help them see that inquiry and challenge and persistence are not soul-sucking activities but opportunities for excitement and discovery.

Early in my teaching career I read the books *You Can't Say You Can't Play* (1992) and *Wally's Stories* (1981) by Vivian Gussin Paley. They were key to developing my understanding of how to teach the whole child. Paley's approach to teaching focused on children's storytelling. She believed that stories and fantasy play help children develop social and emotional skills as well as academic skills such as oral language and reading comprehension. Using the real worries, joys, and questions children have in the classroom, she said, allows them to recognize and negotiate complex issues such as rejection, exclusion, and fairness. Paley used children's stories as the foundation for mini-plays shared at the front of the classroom. These simple dramatizations involved a great deal of dialogue and discussion before, during, and after the play.

These discussions and mini-plays created genuine openings for the students to develop self-control and responsibility. They exhibited self-control when they were respectful audience members and when they followed directions as actors in the play. The students took responsibility by making revisions to their stories so they would be clearly understood and by making sure each of their classmates had an opportunity to tell a story.

Over the years, Paley's child-centered approach to teaching and learning has been challenged by those who prefer more authoritarian practices and direct instruction. I've often heard from new teachers who say they are afraid to let young students play as part of their learning, particularly in the age of high-stakes testing. As a new teacher, I once shared their concerns. I wasn't ready then to make storytelling a central feature of my instruction, but as I grew more confident in my classroom management skills and in my ability to adapt the curriculum, I realized the power of listening deeply to children's personal lives to support their reading and writing.

As often as possible, I try to encourage peer-to-peer dialogue instead of having students respond primarily to the teacher's questions. In other words, I try to get out of their way. My goal is to set up situations where the content flows around students so they have to use it. I believe that the more authentic we make their need to express themselves and be understood, the better they learn. If they can be successful orally and through play, then it makes it easier when they're reading, writing, and communicating.

CONVEYING EMOTIONS IN OUR WRITING

To prepare the children to dramatize their stories, we learn to notice how an author shows emotion, such as through the use of bold text, different font sizes, exclamation points, and ellipses, which change the way we read and think about the words. We learn to alter our voices to match what the characters are feeling.

We also discuss how paying attention to these clues from the author can help us understand the story better.

To develop this process further we tell Tiny Toy Tales. These delightful dramatizations from Sean Layne of Focus Five Inc. (www.artsintegrationcon-sulting.com) use small figurines, simple scripts, and specific movements to tell a classic story. *The Giant Pumpkin*, based on *The Giant Carrot* by Jan Peck, is one of our favorite tales and teaches the life cycle of the pumpkin while introducing students to the features of great storytelling. In telling the tale, the students must change their voices to fit the characters' intonations. They also must use specific motions to match the characters' different personalities and speak with fluency and inflection to make the story interesting.

For Writing Workshop, I model on large paper how to tell and retell a story before picking up a pencil to write it. I explain to the children that the reason we are telling the story across the blank pages is that we want readers to be able to see the story in their heads and feel the story in their hearts. In order to do this, we must be able to see and feel it in our heads and hearts too. Then I let them teach themselves how to put the parts of a story on each page.

I focus on "real and true and happened to you" stories because these personal narratives provide great depth for teaching editing and revision skills. Although I respect my students as authors and honor their choices about what to write, I draw the line at stories that merely repeat what children may have seen in the movies or on television. When a student wants to write Spider-Man stories day after day, for example, I say no and I don't feel bad about it. I might tell him, "That's a fun story, but it's not real, and today I want to learn about you. Tell me about your new bike (or old bike or favorite birthday), anything that is real life."

I believe that a student who is stuck on drawing and writing about movie or television characters is scared of trying, scared that his life isn't interesting, or scared he can't draw or spell well. I want to honor his interests, but if my goal is to inspire and challenge him, I cannot let him believe those negative things about himself. I must teach him to identify his interests and not let him default to "safe" (predictable and boring) stories. The truth is, he already knows Spider-Man is not his story. He has no real connection to it, no emotional investment in the product.

When deciding on topics for writing, some students will struggle. I almost always have at least one student who stubbornly tells me she did nothing over the weekend before returning to school. "Nothing?! You slept in your bed all weekend and never once got up to eat or use the bathroom?" I ask in mock horror. By encouraging and observing my students throughout the day I can usually find a topic that sparks at least mild interest for writing. With some probing (and sometimes "forcing"), I can usually shift a student's thinking, not just about the focus of the story but also about the major reason we write—to share and communicate a message.

CHARACTER DEVELOPMENT

To strengthen the purpose of writing, I also conference with my young authors to help them think about character development. This sounds like a sophisticated process, but it arises naturally during our talks and usually consists of my encouraging them to add a line of dialogue or a description of an emotion. Although I do not *require* them to include these things in their work, I point out how doing so would help the reader better understand the story. Kathleen Fay, my literacy collaborative coach, helped me learn to "teach the poet, not the poem." To me, this means teachers shouldn't insist that students add a specific line to a poem or story, one we think would make the writing perfect. Rather, we should teach students to think critically about their own writing and make adjustments independently, without seeking the teacher's approval. Our goal should be to encourage students to notice and be aware of character development, letting their characters come alive through dialogue and description rather than tying them to the teacher's ideas.

Recalling Paley's work with story dramatization, I decided to use mini-plays to help students probe their characters' thoughts and emotions. The whole class gets involved in these short portrayals, and thus the storyteller, actors, and audience all have a vested interest in the process of questioning, revising, and inferring. In this way, students come to understand that writing is a "message-getting meaning-making activity" (Clay 1991, 6).

DRAMATIZING STORIES

When the children's writing folders are bursting with entries, we learn to sort them into three piles: finished, not finished, and ready for drama. From the "ready for drama" pile, students choose one story they would like to publish (rewrite and bind for the classroom library). As they read their chosen works during our Author Share, the rest of us ask, "How would that look in real life?"

Our familiarity with Tiny Toy Tales gives us a foundation for dramatizing stories, and now we apply these techniques when sharing our own stories. These shows are not elaborate productions. The children use only the simplest of props when necessary, and each show lasts about ten minutes. The learning will come from the discussions, the questions, the clarifications, not from the final product. No one but us will see these mini-plays, and I try to have every child produce at least two plays during this unit. We act out parts of each story, adding movements and dialogue, with the author's directions. The students talk with and listen to one another as we learn about staying on topic and identifying important events

This was Abigail's written story, one of my favorites: "My baby breaks my crayons. I say no baby. My mom say no baby. My baby breaks my crayons more." I called Abigail up to the front and she read her story. The class commiserated; many of them also have baby brothers or sisters who mess with their things. We discussed how many characters were in her play, and Abigail pulled three sticks from the name jar to select the actors for her show.

"Marcos, you be me and sit over here. Andrew, you be the baby and sit here. And Virginia, you be my mom and be in the kitchen over there," Abigail directed. The actors moved to their assigned spots while Abigail turned to the rest of the class. She asked the questions we had been practicing:

- "What is the problem in my story?"

- "How does the character fix the problem?"

- "How is the character feeling in my story?"

Abigail called on Eric, who asked for clarification. "Your baby is breaking your crayons, and you tell your mom and you both tell your baby no?"

I interjected, "You're right, Eric, they are trying to fix the problem. Can you show me, without words, how they might tell the baby no?" Some children wagged their fingers, some shook their heads back and forth, and some stuck their hands up like a traffic cop. Abigail nodded in agreement and asked the last question, "How is the character feeling in my story?" A flurry of answers, "Mad," "Sad," "Bad," and I asked Abigail if she felt any of those things. She emphatically said "All three" and declared she would add those details to her story.

Abigail began directing the actors. "Marcos, start coloring and Andrew, crawl over to him and break the crayons." As she spoke, Marcos scribbled on the carpet as Andrew crawled over to him. After giggles from the audience, I heard Brian quietly say she should put the crayons up higher. Abigail recited, "I was coloring. My baby breaks my crayons." She leaned over and whispered to Marcos, "Marcos, shake your finger at the baby and tell him no." Marcos followed her directions ("Look madder, Marcos") and Andrew kept pretending to break the crayons.

"I tell my mom." Again, Abigail leaned over and said to Marcos, "Go tell my mom the baby is breaking the crayons." She continued reciting her story, "and my mom tells the baby no too."

Virginia, doing her best mom imitation, dried her hands and came over to Andrew. "No, Baby!" she said, shaking her head and her finger back and forth. Abigail said to Virginia, "Not so mean. My mom said it nice." And Virginia tried again, "No, no, Baby." Abigail was now giggling, but with a quiet reminder that she had to end her story, she said, "I was really mad." ("Marcos, look more madder. Put your hands on your hips, like this. That's good.") "I go play in my room. The End."

After the applause, we talked to the director about her play. We asked questions ("Does your baby break the crayons a lot?"), we pointed out details Abigail added that helped us ("You told us you went to your room"), and we brainstormed titles Abigail could use to entice the reader to read her play ("Crayon Baby"). I had snapped photos during the play and Abigail used them to publish her play for our classroom library later that week.

READING IS THINKING

These mini-plays strengthen many aspects of our reading and writing work. We think about the characters' emotions, we think about the logical sequence of the plot, we think about the inferences we make when we read and write. We have all had a student who barreled through a text, sounding out words and ignoring punctuation only to look up when we asked them to tell us what happened first and say "Huh?"

A colleague at Bailey's, Steve Miner, creates a large bold poster with his second graders every year that simply says, "Reading Is Thinking" (see Figure 10.2). I love that message! It is so easy to get caught up in Guided Reading levels, how many high-frequency words students know, or what their reading rate is, but mostly I want them to slow down and think about what they are reading and writing. Reading (and writing) is thinking, and being a director of a play has been a fun way to show students just how much thinking goes into communicating and understanding stories.

Teaching literacy using mini-plays builds self-control and responsibility in many ways. Self-control is a skill all students will need in every classroom, job, and personal relationship they have throughout life. It starts with being aware of our thoughts before speaking. The plays show students how to control their thoughts and actions by being both a director and an actor. They learn that responsibility means being held accountable for their choices (as directors) and the consequences of their actions (as actors). Each skill builds on the other and allows students to practice self-control and responsibility (as well as revision, fluency, comprehension, and critical thinking) in an engaging and creative way.

Figure 10.2

A simple poster carries a powerful message.

Chapter 11

PERSEVERANCE

*P*erseverance is defined by Webster's Dictionary (www.m-w.com) as the "continued effort to do or achieve something despite difficulties, failure, or opposition." Difficulties, failures, and oppositions are exactly what everyone faces when learning anything, regardless of age, grade, or background. We must explicitly teach our students that they will stumble and struggle during the year and that when they do, being resilient and determined is more important than getting it right the first time.

In Friendship Workshop I use read-alouds to discuss perseverance. Some books I like are *Thank You, Mr. Falkner* by Patricia Polacco, *Brave Irene* by William Steig, and *Down the Road* by Alice Schertle. These books are great springboards for discussing how the characters set a goal, stumbled in their attempts, readjusted their goals sometimes, and never gave up trying. *Brave Irene* is an especially fun book to read because the lesson of perseverance is so easy to identify, and the children love the main character's determination. I reference the book throughout the year, such as calling one of my students "Brave Maria" or telling another to "Be brave, Brian," when he is frustrated by a math problem or science experiment.

In *Down the Road*, the lesson is about knowing there are people who love and support you even when you fail. Our discussions always bring us closer together as a school family. The main character, Hetty, is finally big enough to go to the store by herself to get eggs for tomorrow's breakfast. Hetty is thrilled to be considered responsible enough to help the family. On the way home from the store, Hetty spies apples in the tree and wants to pick some for her parents. As she stretches to reach the juiciest apple, however, the eggs topple and crash on the ground. Schertle's words capture every child's fear of disappointing a parent. The ending of the book brings a twist and helps us brainstorm creative ways of fixing problems.

Our first Friendship Workshop lesson in perseverance actually takes place in September. I take my students out to the monkey bars on the playground and tell them that for many kindergarten and first-grade students, traveling across the full row of monkey bars is just not possible; they are inexperienced and have not developed the necessary muscles yet. As a class we share our hopes and dreams about being able to scoot across them someday. (Those children who can already cross the bars share how they learned and I suggest they can help their friends learn.) I tell them I believe they will all make it across, but likely at different times and on different days.

We talk about trying the monkey bars every day so they will get stronger and develop more stamina with practice. I explain that they don't have to play on the bars for the whole recess but if they attempt to cross at least once a day they will soon reach their goal. Some days, I tell them, it may feel hard to hold on; that's normal. Some days they might not feel like doing the monkey bars at all; that's normal too. Some days they will want to give up because it seems like everyone else can cross the bars; that's also normal. I tell them together we will figure out new ways to practice, learn from one another, and celebrate when others get across before we do. If they will work hard and believe they will be successful they can become monkey bar experts! (See Abigail demonstrating her monkey bar prowess in Figure 11.1.)

Figure 11.1
Abigail's perseverance pays off as she glides across the monkey bars.

We make a chart in the classroom titled Monkey Bar Progress, and the children delight in coloring the lines that represent their advancements. (It's true that all students will not make it across by the end of the school year, but nearly everyone will achieve developmental milestones.) It's our first introduction to goal setting, self-assessment, and accepting our differences. Later I use the monkey bars as an analogy for our academic perseverance. When studying the high-frequency words, for example, I tell the students they need to practice every day. Some days they might not remember all the words, and some days they may need a new way to practice spelling but they can never give up. Just as with the monkey bars, they must work hard and believe in themselves, and every time they practice their words they will get stronger and smarter.

"ALL PROBLEMS ARE SOLVABLE."

Recently a teacher shared with me how he teaches perseverance to his third graders. In September he shares a video clip from YouTube that shows two people riding an upward escalator. Suddenly the escalator jolts forward and stops. The man in front sighs heavily in disbelief. The woman behind him looks about frantically, checks her watch, and looks around again. The man turns and asks the woman, "Can you believe this? I can't believe this." He then shouts to no one in particular, "Hello!? There are two people stuck on this escalator . . . Hello? We need help!" The woman is in a panic after checking her phone and finding the battery is dead. "What are we going to do?" she agonizes aloud. Eventually a repairman is seen at the floor below them and reassures the two passengers that he will be right up to fix the problem . . . until his escalator jolts forward and stops. As the scene fades out, the three people are seen sitting down on the escalator stairs, resigned to being stuck until someone comes and fixes the problem.

The teacher explained to me that his students loved the video and they all had a good chuckle about the ridiculousness of it—"It's a staircase, for goodness' sake!" one of his students said. Then the teacher explained his real purpose in showing it to them. "You can always help yourself. All problems are solvable." As a class they shared times when they have felt helpless but were able to persevere through the difficulty. Most stories, the teacher told me, revolved around physical trials (such as in sports or on the playground) but through their discussions the children came to see how it applied to social and emotional situations too (such as arguing over who uses the computer first or when you feel left out of a group).

When I was visiting this teacher's classroom in April, a student came up to us and said, "My laptop won't let me log on." The teacher replied, "Are you stuck on an escalator?" and the boy smiled and said, "No, I'll shut it down and try a different one." Clearly the lesson had stuck: "You can always help yourself. All problems are solvable." I cannot wait to show that video next year!

TEACHER LANGUAGE

Responsive Classroom introduced me to the importance of "teacher language," the positive and professional "use of words and tone of voice to enable students to learn in an engaged and active way" (Responsive Classroom 2012). Teacher language conveys our belief in students as capable and responsible contributors to our classroom communities, and it is critical in teaching perseverance. Our language choices "convey our assumptions and expectations about children, which, in turn, influence children's assumptions and expectations about themselves" (2012). Through our words we determine whether the focus is on the product or the process, the student's satisfaction or the teacher's approval, the emergence of new learning or the regurgitation of generic facts. For example, if I say, "I like the way you are staying in your seat, Josue," I am focusing on my approval of Josue doing what I want. If I change my words to instead say, "By staying in your seat you already have six math problems finished. Great focus, Josue!" I help my student understand the expected behavior and the direct impact it has on his success.

When I was a new teacher, I got in the habit of praising my young students in the hopes that others would follow suit. I used to say, "I like the way Jacqueline is sitting with her voice off" and think it would also remind Josue what he should be doing. But that's not what happened! Josue did not connect to generic praise (if he even heard the message) and worse, he found it insulting to be routinely compared to the "teacher's pet." Sometimes students used my praise to later make fun of the child I had cited for exemplary behavior.

In her book *The Power of Our Words*, Paula Denton explains that she also used to praise students into compliance. She writes, "I was trying to manipulate the other students to do what I wanted without them being conscious of my control over them" (2007, 14). Hidden agendas and controlling language never work for teachers because they are temporary and ineffective methods that do not build student autonomy or help them develop intrinsic motivation. In the book, Denton has five guidelines for teacher language:

1. Be direct and genuine.

2. Convey faith in children's abilities and intentions.

3. Focus on action.

4. Keep it brief.

5. Know when to keep silent. (2007, 12)

Although all five are valuable to keep in mind, the two that had the most impact on my teaching are conveying faith in children's intentions and staying focused on the action. I use these principles to keep myself in check when a situation becomes unusually frustrating. They keep me calm and mindful and remind me that the situation is temporary (the student *wants* to act appropriately) and fixable (the action can be redirected).

When a student misbehaves, I must communicate that I trust that her intention was good and simply misguided and not a calculated or malicious action. This belief is vital in helping a student see herself as capable of the appropriate behavior as well as capable of making a change. Rita Piersen, an educator with forty years' experience, said in a TED talk, "Every child deserves a champion—an adult who will never give up on them, who understands the power of connection, and insists that they become the best that they can possibly be" (2013). Perseverance instills in students the internal motivation to insist that they become the best they can be.

The second guideline I follow is focusing on the action, because it helps me remain objective and neutral regarding the student's behavior. Rather than rolling my eyes and accusing the student of intentionally interrupting the lesson, I simply state the error and the expected behavior (or consequence). Focusing on the action allows me to remain relaxed and calm in my body language and tone of voice, and this helps the student to feel respected and less defensive. These two guidelines for language choice set the stage for students' self-talk to be optimistic and helpful rather than pessimistic and defeating.

Figure 11.2 shows a graphic representation of the reflective process that I go through as I consider the possible causes of students' misbehaviors, observe their interpersonal relationships, and think of actions I could take to address their social and emotional needs in terms of perseverance and then to redirect their behavior. In the following section, I explore different sets of teacher reflections related to the Friendship Workshop topic of perseverance and discuss examples of how students' interactions might play out in the classroom.

"I'M DONE!"

Teachers everywhere have struggled with students who complete an assignment too rapidly to be believed. We all know what's up when a student calls out, "I'm done!" almost as soon as she's started.

Seventeen years of teaching experience have informed my prediction that students will need about twenty minutes to complete the activity I assign on this day, yet Yancy invests a mere three minutes before shouting out, "I'm done!" She looks around the room with an expression that is both triumphant and mischievous. I know that what I do in response will be critical to Yancy's development, but it also will be important for the other students, who are silently wondering why they should stick with the hard work when one of their peers has bailed out with minimal effort.

We are well beyond the beginning of the school year when students may fail to finish because they are still learning our classroom routines or developing stamina for academic work, so I know that Yancy has merely made a hasty pass at the assignment and probably also made many mistakes along the way. For students like Yancy, we must communicate the belief that they are capable of meeting higher expectations and then identify specific and concrete ways that they can persevere with an assignment. Above all, we want to avoid getting into a power struggle with our students by playing the role of the enforcer or compliance cop, which undermines trust and may lead to other misbehaviors.

Behaviors

Speed demon (rushes through work)

Procrastination   Self-defeating attitude

Unwillingness to try   Fidgeting

Reflection Questions

When does it occur?   With whom?

What exactly is the student doing?

Does the student finish anything?

During what time of day or subject does it happen?

Does the student know the expectations?

Is the student cautious about most activities?

Does the student feel
defeated easily?

Possible Needs

Learn accountability   Feel powerful or successful

Trust that it is okay to make mistakes

Time-management tools   Self-confidence

Learn that growth happens over time

Figure 11.2
Developing
Perseverance

Reflection Questions

Does she rush through every subject or just specific ones? Does she attempt the work or apply any effort? Do specialist teachers (music, art) see the same behavior in their classrooms?

Possible Needs

Finishing first makes some students feel powerful. Because they are familiar with images of winning—the Super Bowl, an Olympic gold medal, the checkered flag at a NASCAR race—some children will falsely announce they are finished just to feel successful, even if it's only temporary (because they usually have made careless mistakes or forgotten to complete the second page and then have to return to their desks to complete the assignment correctly). There's nothing wrong with wanting to be a winner—believe me, as a competitive gymnast I loved coming in first—but in the classroom we need to create an atmosphere that lets students feel victorious in many ways. Rather than only praising the first person to cross the finish line, we must also encourage and celebrate those who invest effort, engage in the process of learning, and emphasize quality over speed.

Possible Actions

A verbal reminder can often help those speed demon finishers. When handing out the assignment, we can use a simple check-in to refocus the student. I pulled Yancy aside and said, "Yancy, tell me what you will be doing during math in three steps." (I use three steps because students can easily remember them.)

Yancy said, "I will get the bears for making my graph, I will work on all five questions, and I will raise my hand when I am done."

"Great," I told her. "I will come to you in ten minutes. You keep working until I come over." This simple reminder can then be used to reinforce Yancy's effort ("You're doing what you said, Yancy. Way to be responsible!") or used for accountability ("Yancy, how many problems did you say you would work on? Show me").

"I'M NOT FINISHED!"

Reflection Questions

What about students who never finish on time? Are they too busy socializing? Have they developed "learned helplessness," a condition that causes them to feel insecure and incapable of independent action? Are they wandering the classroom, or are they quietly disengaged from the activity?

Possible Needs

I find that procrastinators are usually too busy socializing or craftily avoiding the work because it's too hard. These students may need a better understanding of their specific job during work time, or they may need a different explanation of the assignment so they aren't confused about the expectations. Breaking the activity into small steps can help them progress without feeling overwhelmed. Some children may need a direct reward after completing an activity (or behavior) in order to build stamina and accountability.

It seems rewards are always a tricky subject matter for teachers—do they help or hurt students? Do they motivate or create dependence on outside approval? For me, it comes down to what I am hoping to gain from implementing the reward. For the student to become better at *x, y,* or *z,* I want the reward to be quick and easy and implemented for only a brief time. The reward must connect directly to the outcome. For example, if my goal for a student is to be more invested in learning, then a reward of extra recess doesn't make sense. But reading her story to the front office staff directly connects to investing more effort during Writing Workshop.

Possible Actions

Checklists are a great way to help students become accountable for their learning. Checklists also provide visual cues for students who need them. When designing checklists, I break down the skills, build in small breaks for the student to move about, and then have her check her progress. The breaks are the same (get a drink of water, sharpen a pencil) and the components are small (five minutes of reading or four problems in math), but each break requires a self-assessment when the student returns to work—perhaps a check mark next to the time frame or a circle around a mistake. Each part builds stamina and confidence as well as self-awareness of success.

"IS THIS ENOUGH?"

Reflection Questions

Does the student do as little as possible on all assignments? Does he produce the minimum amount of work required and then stop? When I announce, "You need to have at least three sentences," does he focus on the requirement and lose sight of the purpose? Does he feel incapable of more work, or is he unsure of what "more" looks like?

Possible Needs

Learned helplessness in its most tragic forms usually stems from a repeated and significant trauma such as physical or verbal abuse. But even a single exposure to a negative situation can make the brain rewire itself in defense (Jensen 2009). At the heart of learned helplessness is a sense of having no control in a situation. If a student has experienced repeated put-downs, he may adapt by giving up control in all areas as a defense against the negative feeling.

Possible Actions

Martin Seligman's book *Learned Optimism* (2006) is an excellent resource for helping students develop perseverance and resiliency. Some of Seligman's techniques are methods teachers already do in the classroom. For example, when students feel defeated, Seligman suggests externalizing their voices. I call this process self-talk and use it to reframe students' negative thoughts. When Kelly constantly blames the book for being too hard, I might reframe her words to reflect the temporary difficulty: "Today this book feels too hard. You read this page and then we can pick a different book." When José is convinced there is only one outcome (failing) to his trying the math worksheet, I might help him find alternatives: "José, if you try these, then (1) you might get them right and we will celebrate, (2) you might get some wrong and we will fix them together, (3) your desk might turn into an alien spaceship and you'll lift off to Mars." (The silly alternative always shifts the mood and can dissolve the intensity of the student's fears.)

LITERACY CONNECTION: PERSEVERANCE AND GIVING AND GETTING FEEDBACK CONNECT TO READING AND WRITING NONFICTION AND PRESENTING

Our nonfiction work comes in the early spring when students are comfortable working collaboratively and independently, sharing their ideas and listening to new ones, asking for help and helping others. We have been reading nonfiction texts in Reading Workshop and in Science and Math Workshops and biographies in our social studies period, so the genre of nonfiction is not new to students. We now look closely at the differences in the text features of fiction and nonfiction and make charts outlining what we notice. The bold fonts, the photographs and captions, and the fun facts all intrigue the students, and they begin to see how they can read a nonfiction book even when they don't know all the words. We discuss how a good nonfiction book, like a good work of fiction, leaves us with an emotional response, with questions, with a desire to read more.

Writing Workshop begins with a lesson I learned from my friend and colleague Melissa Fleischer. I bring in the stack of books I keep next to my bed: *The Heart of the Buddha's Teachings* (Thich Nhat Hahn 1998), *Smithsonian* magazine, Nelson Mandela's (1995) autobiography, and *The Essentials of Science and Literacy* (Worth et al. 2009). I tell my students that these books are teaching me about things I want to learn. I also explain that each of them can teach me as well. For example, Valerie knows how to draw a hopscotch board. Amner can make the best tacos (because he told me his mom does). And Nikki can swim underwater. These are all things I would love to learn more about! We spend a few days discussing and making lists of skills and knowledge we could teach other people.

Our next step is to make book covers, which show all the things we know about our subjects in illustrated form. In the past, some students would say they wanted to write an "All About" book on a certain topic (turtles, for example), but a day or two into the project they would have little information and less interest in the topic. By focusing on the drawings and the conversations that revolve around the topic, we can deepen students' knowledge and help them determine which subjects they want to take to the writing stage. After working on the covers, the students pick one topic to write about and publish. We discuss that this book will need to teach people, so their work must be factual, detailed, and interesting.

The reading and writing lessons link beautifully to our Friendship Workshop focus on perseverance. Through revision and editing, students learn to go back and check their facts, rewrite pages to be more precise with the data, and add detailed illustrations and captions to help readers learn about their chosen topics. Each revision is an opportunity to teach students accountability, determination, and self-satisfaction in a job well done. We read our books to each other, other classes, and staff members (see the school secretary Mrs. Sisk reading with a student in Figure 11.3).

Students share their work regularly with one another in pairs, small groups, or whole groups at the end of Writing Workshop, but our favorite style of presenting is when we go on "book tour." These book tours can be formal or spontaneous and always bring pride and joy to the students. When the presentations are formal scheduled events, we write invitations to our families and school staff members and ask them to come to our room at a specific time to hear our stories.

To prepare, students spend two or three days finishing their illustrations, creating a cover, and practicing reading their story. To get the room ready, we spread out the chairs randomly in groups of two. When the start time rolls around, each student sits in one of the chairs and leaves the other chair open for visitors. They have their stories with them, but they also have their book box to read from while they wait. They read quietly until a grown-up comes and sits down. The student author says, "Hello, my name is _____. What's your name?" and "Would you like to hear my story?"

When the student is finished reading, he or she asks, "Do you have any questions or comments for me?" and they relish answering questions and giving more details to the listener. When the adult is finished and thank-yous have been exchanged, the adult moves on to another chair, another author, another story. When the time is up and everyone has left, the class sits together and shares a special snack with iced tea or lemonade as we bubble over with stories about who came to listen to us.

I love this style of presenting because there is no pressure—on the students or me! There is no spotlight on one reader as the other students fidget and become nervous waiting for their turn. There is a quiet buzz in the room that helps the students speak clearly (as opposed to mumbling through the deafening silence when it's one speaker at a time), and there is an easy flow in the room as the adults move from chair to chair, allowing students multiple opportunities to share their story. With each telling, the students become more comfortable and more confident in their identity as an author. I personally delight in watching the joy spread across a student's face when a grown-up sits down and asks, "Can I hear your story?"

Sometimes, our tours are totally spontaneous because I am so energized by the students' talents! These tours are not completed stories, they are not rehearsed presentations, and they usually happen on a Friday afternoon (imagine that!). I e-mail two or three fellow teachers and ask if the students can come by for a few minutes to share their works in progress. I ask them to prep their students to ask questions such as "What will you add to your story next?" "How will you illustrate your story?" or "What is the ending?" I also ask them to let their students make suggestions to the authors. This keeps the focus on the process of writing (not a finished product) and helps the students (in both groups) practice planning, clarifying, and revising in an authentic way.

The teachers arrange the chairs in their room in groups of two, and this time the authors move from seat to seat. (This took some coaching with my kindergartners—sitting next to a big fourth grader can be intimidating!—but after a few tours almost every student loves looking for a new audience.) We spend maybe seven minutes in each class, and then we're off to the next room. Two or three presentations later, we gather back in our room to share the ideas they got from the other students. These tours bring a lot of energy back to the Writing Workshop—not just that day but for a few weeks afterward—and

Figure II.3
Leonel shares his story about going to the carnival with our office secretary, Mrs. Sisk.

they remind us all that writing is a communication tool that connects us to one another.

Part of our discussion afterward is about the process of writing and the perseverance it takes to become an expert in the topic.

SMALL STEPS, BIG GAINS

There are many stories of perseverance in every classroom. They may seem small and insignificant in the grand scheme of things: Johnny learns to write his name in kindergarten, Ezequiel learns to tell time in first grade, and Virginia understands how to count money in second grade. Yet most teachers will agree that the accumulation of these small steps enables students to make big gains by the time they advance to the next grade.

My favorite story of perseverance has to do with Oscar, a Spanish speaker whose parents had only completed the fifth grade in their native Guatemala. They both worked two jobs and yet still found time to take Oscar to the library and the park and into Washington, D.C., on their days off (which wasn't often). Although these outings might seem simple and obvious to many of us, they were not easy to accomplish for people of limited means who didn't speak, read, or write English. But Oscar's parents loved him and were determined to help him be successful in school.

In our classroom, Oscar was polite and somewhat unanimated, meaning I was never quite sure what he was getting from my lessons. He would participate in discussions sporadically and he could just as easily play with friends as without them. He was very comfortable with numbers and geometry but struggled with letters and words. He loved books about the ocean, sharks in particular, and could draw several species with good detail. To help him learn English his parents diligently sang the ABCs, used the flash cards I made for him, and "read" to him every night before bed. Oscar's parents told me they worried they could not help him learn to read or write because they did not know English. I explained to them that reading books in their native language is a valuable way to support his reading progress. I also showed them how to "read" a book written in English by using the pictures (without reading the words) and how to discuss the story together. I shared how these conversations would help them strengthen Oscar's fluency, story sequencing, and comprehension.

Each quarter I described Oscar's progress in anecdotal form on the progress report but each quarter I also had to mark down that he was still below grade-level expectations.

In January of that school year, Oscar's demeanor seemed to change. He became quieter and more of a loner at recess. During Reading Workshop Oscar became more and more frustrated with his difficulties. He would stomp away from a spelling center, put his head down during our guided reading group, and turn his body away during read-alouds. When I checked in with his parents, I discovered that a new baby brother was disrupting Oscar's home routine. His parents, as all new parents do, had less time for Oscar, who felt left out. I invited his mom to come after school with the baby once a week for reading time. She would watch Oscar and me read together and work on letters and words, and then she would take the lessons home with her. Although their time together at home was still limited, his mom's visits to school boosted Oscar's spirit.

I began making books for Oscar to take home to read to the baby. These were simple, one- or two-word books with a picture, but Oscar treasured those books. During class he started searching for other simple books he could read to his brother. His spelling sessions now consisted of five minutes of the required words for the class and five minutes of the words *brother*, *love*, and *Carlos* (his brother's name). Oscar began to see words in the school hallway and on posters that he recognized. He also began to see them in read-alouds and in his guided reading texts.

One day in late April, I was working with another student, Jason, at a round table (I can picture this moment so vividly) when something clicked for Oscar. It was Reading Workshop center time and there was a bustle about the room as children worked in pairs, spelling words, playing memory games, or writing words on the chalkboard. Oscar was alone, at the back of the room, poring over a new guided reading text. As Jason started to read his book to me, Oscar suddenly appeared, plopped the book down on the table, and interrupted us, saying, "Ms. Buckley! The words . . . they came down . . . I can read!" He raised his hands into the air, waving them around his head to indicate that the words that had been "up there" were now in the book that he held in front of him. Everything now made sense to him! He proudly read the entire book to me, *Wake Up, Dad* by Beverley Randell (1995), and I hooted and hollered and ran down the hall and made him read to every teacher we met, including Emelie Parker and Tess Pardini, who used Oscar's phrase for the title of their book, *The Words Came Down* (2006).

Watching the light go on in a new reader's mind is never a small moment in a teacher's career, but this moment, for me, was the ultimate validation that learning is an accumulation of small steps and processes. It takes time and hard work, persistence and faith, flexibility and determination—perseverance. As an educator I must instill these qualities in my students along with the unwavering belief that they are capable, they are resilient, and they will be successful.

Chapter 12

GIVING AND GETTING FEEDBACK

Feedback happens all the time. As I get ready for work my sweetie says, "You look nice," and I feel more confident. The Starbucks barista recommends a new drink based on my craving for the day. Valerie tells Nikki she will play puppies at recess but *only* if Valerie can be the mother pup this time. Feedback is how we weigh our options, make decisions, and negotiate our day. Giving and getting productive feedback in the academic realm is an essential quality of an engaged learner.

I introduce my first lesson about feedback during snack time. I have pretzels and graham crackers. After the children make their choices, I ask them to look around. Something is clearly wrong, I tell them. "Emma has graham crackers and Bella has pretzels! How can they be friends anymore?" After three or four other silly examples (Amner has a Spider-Man T-shirt on today and Marcos is wearing Angry Birds—they can't be friends, can they?), the class gets what I'm saying—it's okay to like different things.

Next I use P. D. Eastman's book, *Go, Dog. Go!* (1961), which features a dog that asks another dog if he likes her hat. He does not. I use this narrative to start a discussion about respecting differences. We talk about how the first dog changes her hat and asks the same question over and over. She doesn't stop wearing hats, she doesn't stop trying different hats, she doesn't really seem to mind that the other dog doesn't like her hat; she simply asks the question and tries something new. We each take a strip of plain paper to make a headband and we ask, "Do you like my hat?" We practice answering in a respectful way, "No, I do not like your hat."

Next, each using the same headband, we add a decoration (pom-pom, glitter, stickers—anything from that giant box of stuff all teachers have in their classrooms) and ask again, "Do you like my hat?" After several additions to our hats and several rounds of politely answering, "No, I do not like your hat" (even if we do) we finish the lesson by learning the reply, "That's okay. I do." We take a group photo of our silly hats and post it with the words "I like my hat!" This final step lets students know that it is okay to have strong preferences and to not feel rejected if someone doesn't share your view.

One year I used art prints for a lesson. I showed the selected prints on the overhead projector for a whole-class viewing. I chose dark, dreary, abstract prints such as Vincent van Gogh's *The Potato Eaters* or Jackson Pollack's *Zeichnung Tropftechnik*. I asked if anyone liked these prints. Most of the children said no because of the unexciting colors or depressing expressions. Next, I displayed some vibrant upbeat prints such as Van Gogh's *Starry Night* or Wassily Kandinsky's *Merry Structure*, and almost all students shouted in agreement that they liked these prints.

I went back to the original *Potato Eaters* print and told the students, "I wouldn't want this in my house, but I do like the way the light shines down on their faces. Does anyone else see one part they like?" A few students said they liked the teapot or the little girl, and Scarlett said she liked the lady giving the potato because there probably wasn't a lot of food and she was sharing. "It's a little bit of hope," she said. (Ahh, Scarlett, my poet; I miss her.) Referencing the Pollack piece, some students said that maybe they saw a swimmer in the left corner, or maybe it was a snake in the right corner, and they liked that. I used these comments to explain that often when we don't like something we can usually still find one nice thing to say about it.

We looked at more prints and took turns saying, "I do not like the print but I do like _____ [the blue lines, the little boy, the water shining, and so on]." I explained that when we point out the one part we do like, we are giving feedback to the artists, and these comments can help them become better (at art or writing or singing). This is how we can disagree politely with one another. Explicitly teaching students how to observe work and make at least one positive comment establishes an atmosphere of respect and kindness that will make it easier for students during peer conferences, where they will practice giving and getting feedback about their own work.

Giving feedback requires us to be kind, responsible, and accepting of different ideas, skills we have been developing all year long. But first, we must learn to extend those kindnesses to ourselves.

As we get feedback about the quality of our work, we learn to self-evaluate our reading and writing. Not everything we draw or write will be great, and evaluating the work and not the person is an important concept to learn. We explore feeling satisfied with our work as well as not feeling proud of our work. We are reminded of our "self-talk" skills and practice silently. We might look at our writing and ask ourselves (and eventually each other) questions such as "Does it make sense?" and "Do my illustrations help the reader?" In math we might ask, "Was I clear in my explanation?" and "Does my work show every step in solving it?" We are specific and positive with our words and learn to choose one thing to change or improve. We learn the importance of phrases such as "Thanks for the idea" and "Maybe next time I'll try that."

THE FEAR OF FEEDBACK

Type "Am I good enough?" into a computer search engine and you get nine billion results! It seems that many of us struggle with this universal question, and young children are no different. Their defense mechanisms for avoiding criticism or culpability for their mistakes tend to be more obvious than adults': they blame the pencil for not being sharp enough, the teacher for being mean or, most famously, the dog for eating their homework, but in essence they are trying to escape the sensation of feeling bad about themselves. Hearing negative feedback can hurt our hearts, and over time we can believe we are no good.

Tara Brach, a clinical psychologist and meditation teacher, writes, "Feeling 'not good enough' is that often unseen engine that drives our daily behavior and life choices" (2014). Brach explains that we frequently become fixated on a singular negative incident while forgetting the larger expanse of positive responses, people, and events we have experienced. I want to help my students understand that we are not defined by one moment in time. My goal is to introduce hearing feedback as a way to improve our skills and decision making in both academic and social situations.

DEFENSE MECHANISMS

Students exhibit a range of behaviors when they get negative feedback, but all the responses seem to stem from the same desire—to deflect feeling bad about themselves.

- Some students use excuses: "My mom forgot to put my homework folder in my backpack." Or "Someone took my reading spot."

- Some students become defensive: "You never told me I had to hand it in today" (while they stare at the chalkboard with the assignment dates clearly written). Or "I tried but everyone is so noisy."

- Some students become accusatory and try to bring in a third party to deflect their responsibility: "Randy started it." Or "Jasmine told me to."

Reflection Questions

Along with the reflection questions I ask about every situation (When does it occur? Does it happen with any particular student?), I ask these two questions when I see students having difficulty with receiving feedback or criticism:

1. Do they regularly blame things outside of their control?

2. Is there any truth to their excuses?

For example, does he blame everyone else for his misfortune or misconduct? Are there times during the day that she does demonstrate feeling capable and in control? Can he identify when he made a good choice and a good outcome occurred (meaning, can he give himself good feedback)?

Possible Needs

Blaming things outside of students' control may indicate that they are feeling frustrated by a lack of power. They may not have much experience with making their own choices or decisions and therefore have learned to blame outside circumstances for their situation. They may need repeated practice in seeing how their actions can lead to positive outcomes before I can expect them to change a behavior based on a negative outcome.

Possible Actions

Young students often need to see direct connections between a decision and a result. Remember Mario, from Chapter 2? I had to dance and sing when he hung up his backpack and walked right to his table for morning work. He may not have actually started his work, but choosing to go to his table and not wander the room or hallway or annoy his peers was a decision and he needed to hear that he had made a positive choice and feel the positive outcome.

I have mentioned before that reinforcing these incidents for selected students can sometimes seem like a lot of energy invested in one child, but for me the payoff is worth it when I reflect on what might be causing the student to misbehave. Before I understood that Mario could not yet balance academic and social skills, I usually got mad at him for not knowing how to make the right choice. I hyperfocused on what he *wasn't* doing. When I became aware of the dichotomy, it felt effortless to give him high fives for sitting quietly for five minutes or a big hug for walking in line quietly. Stopping the class and announcing "Holy moly! Did you guys see that? Mario went right to his morning work! Ain't he awesome?" made Mario feel happy and proud, and his classmates recognized that he was gaining maturity and control in small ways.

LANGUAGE THAT SUPPORTS AUTONOMY

It is important for students to realize that the choice-and-outcome relationship has nothing to do with teacher approval (although they may get a positive response from us when they do make positive choices). In other words, we don't want them to make choices to seek our approval. Brief and precise language from us encourages students to verbalize the connection and helps strengthen their self-regulation skills.

For example, I might say to Anthony, "I see you logged on to the reading site right away. What happens next?"

"I can choose my reading partner."

"That's right. Following directions the first time is why you get to choose your partner. You made a strong choice."

The same, precise language works for the not-so-good choices too.

"Jessica, you are choosing to wander the room instead of getting to work. What happens next?"

"You choose my writing spot."

"That's right. You chose not to get to work on time so you lose your privilege of picking a spot. I will choose it now and tomorrow you can make a stronger choice."

Reflection Question

When students regularly deflect responsibility, I make myself listen carefully to what they are saying. Is there truth to the statement? Does he have an elaborate explanation that skims the surface of the truth without ever admitting responsibility? (My question: "Marcos, did you draw on Sam's paper?" His response: "Well, he was talking about Pokemon and I was telling him how to draw Pikachu and he said no and there was no paper and I had to show him the right way to draw the head.")

Possible Needs

Taking responsibility for our actions is brave. Children who ramble on and on, explaining their perspective and deflecting blame, may need reassurance that mistakes are inevitable—it is what we do *after* making them that matters. They may need to hear the situation described in small nonemotional chunks in order to accept the responsibility for their actions.

Possible Actions

When Sam got upset that Marcos drew on his paper, I was 90 percent certain that Marcos was guilty, mostly because he drew Pikachu *everywhere* and the crayon color matched his. But I needed to have Marcos connect the dots between his choice and the outcome.

"Let me see if I have this right. Sam, you wanted to know how to draw Pikachu, is that right?"

"Yes, but . . . ," Sam starts.

"Hold up," I say, placing my hand on his shoulder. "Let's do this in parts. Sam, you wanted to see how to draw Pikachu, is that right?"

"Yes," Sam answers.

"Marcos, you wanted to help, is that right?" (This acknowledges that Marcos's intention was to be helpful.)

"Yes," he says. "I know how to draw it because I have a book at home on how to draw them."

"Great. Sam, do you agree that Marcos wanted to help?" Sam nods his head in agreement.

"Marcos, you chose to draw it on Sam's paper, is that right?"

Marcos shifts his gaze downward and mumbles, "Yes."

"Marcos, did you ask Sam if you could draw it on his paper?"

His head still down, he answers, "Yes."

"Marcos, we can fix this with your friend if we have the truth. Did you ask Sam if you could draw it on his paper?" Marcos shakes his head. "Okay. Thanks. If you had asked Sam, how do you think Sam would feel now?"

"Better . . . ?" Marcos looks up at Sam, hoping he is right.

"Sam, do you think if Marcos had made the choice to ask you to draw on his paper that you would feel better now?"

Sam says, "Yes," and his tone makes it clear that's all he really wanted from Marcos, just to be asked permission.

I restate the situation so both boys understand the positive and negative choices clearly. "So, Sam was looking for help and Marcos wanted to help. He just picked the wrong place to draw it. Does that sound right?"

Both boys look at me and say, "Yes."

"Marcos, can you let Sam know you made a mistake?" Marcos tells Sam he's sorry for drawing on his paper, and I get a clean sheet from the bin to let him show Sam the finer points of Pikachu's head.

As teachers, we strive to have our students manage their choices appropriately and problem-solve independently. Yet I wonder how often we step back and consider how much inner strength that can take for young children. Sometimes becoming involved and offering the clear objective voice of an adult is just the support a student needs to be able to take responsibility for a misdeed.

LITERACY CONNECTION: GIVING AND GETTING FEEDBACK AND PERSEVERANCE CONNECT TO READING AND WRITING NONFICTION, WRITING POETRY, AND PEER CONFERENCES

Peer-to-peer conferences have always been tricky for me. Keeping the student talk focused on the work (as opposed to the latest *SpongeBob* episode), expecting students to give objective feedback (rather than, "I like your picture" praise), and hoping they would be respectful (instead of wielding the red pen like a weapon across each other's work) seemed more troublesome than useful. However, when I realized that feedback was a social/emotional skill I wanted my students to learn, I began to look at peer conferences in the primary grades in a different light. Rather than using them to improve a particular piece of writing, I shifted the focus to understanding (and accepting) that all writing can be improved.

Evaluating and Revising

Our Friendship Workshop lessons on giving and getting feedback coincide with the final phase of our nonfiction unit. As we near the publishing phase, I introduce a rubric to the whole class, using my own book as the example. Throughout the unit, I have been writing alongside the children, modeling in whole-group and in small conferences various nonfiction features. Many of the pages of my book are incomplete because I do not want to leave the impression that the students' books need to mimic mine. These incomplete pages provide the perfect opportunity for the students to make sense of the rubric.

Figure 12.1
Nonfiction Rubric

Each column represents the level of effort the students put into their nonfiction work. The partners discuss their work and then choose a box that reflects their assessment. For example, if the students read three books and looked at two websites, they would give themselves a 3 in the Research column. If they had only one photograph, they would give themselves a 1 for Illustrations.

Name _____   Date _____

Circle the appropriate box for each category.

Effort	Research	Text	Illustrations	Presentation
3	4+ pages Book Web Personal Interview	4+ pages Teaches new facts and information (ex., *There are more than 300 types of dogs.*)	4+ pages Photos or drawings with captions and fun facts	Exciting title Creative layout Neat Colorful
2	3–4 pages Book Web Personal Interview	3–4 pages Basic facts 1 new fact	2–3 pages Photos or drawings with captions	Good title Neat Colorful
1	1–2 pages Book Web Personal Interview	1–2 pages Basic facts (ex., *A dog has 4 legs.*)	1 page Photo or drawing No captions	Plain title Plain cover Plain pages

The rubric breaks down the four components of our nonfiction work: Research, Text, Illustrations, and Presentation (see Figure 12.1). Level One represents a minimal effort and Level Three shows high effort. These components are not based on the state writing standards or grade-level expectations because the point of the lesson is to introduce how to give and receive feedback. The rubric teaches students how to analyze and evaluate their work for specific components. Later, I can add punctuation or spelling or other categories as the children gain strength in using the rubrics effectively.

After several lessons in which I use the rubric to reflect on my book, I assign partners and have the students complete the assessment using each other's work. My aim in these peer conferences is to let students get comfortable hearing from another person how their work is strong or where it needs to be improved. The "I like your book" syndrome is eliminated because the students are only commenting on the four tangible elements.

After the students evaluate their work, we spend time revising and adding to our books, using the specific suggestions from the conferences. Later, we use the rubrics again to see the improvements we made and to feel proud of applying our best efforts.

Most years I will have one or two students who may, on their rough drafts, receive the highest mark on the rubric. I have found that this can work to the benefit of the classroom community because now the other students clearly see how the quality of the excellent work differs from their own, and that there are exact steps they can take to produce the same quality of work if they choose. I have then added components to differentiate for the more advanced students.

Purposeful Poetry

Poetry is so subjective and personal that using a feedback rubric might seem incongruent. But, just as with nonfiction, there are clear and distinct features that students must learn and be able to identify. Using resources such as Lucy Calkins's *Poetry: Powerful Thoughts in Tiny Packages* (2003) and *Climb Inside a Poem* by Georgia Heard and Lester Laminack (2008), I begin our poetry unit by listening—really listening—to poems. I like these particular resources because, while the specific lessons and activities help me introduce writing poems, the books challenge me to think about poetry differently. They almost dare me not to follow the exact words and lessons but rather look and listen deeply to the students in front of me and see that their words, their perspectives, and their insights are so organic and natural that if I will get out of the way I will hear the children creating poems every day.

I read a poem once, and then I ask the students to close their eyes as I read it again. Next, we share whatever stood out for us—words, an image, or the rhyme—and connected to our hearts and imaginations. The students offer a range of insights and we discuss how not all poems connect to all people in the same way. During one discussion, Cynthia, a first grader, said some poems make you feel "strong" inside because your heart likes them so much. Other poems are "fuzzy," Cynthia said, like trying to see underwater. What a wonderful description! I used the words *fuzzy* and *strong* in our poetry rubric (see Figure 12.2) to help students recognize the range of quality from ineffective to effective. The four structural components of the poetry rubric are rhyme, patterns, or sound words; imagery; line breaks; and heart connections (whether the reader feels the emotion).

Figure 12.2
Poetry Rubric

Each column has three levels, with 1 being the least amount of effort and 3 being the most. The students reflect on the poem and choose a level that matches their effort. (For example, in Graciela's draft poem, she and her partner decided on a 2 for Imagery and Line Breaks and a 1 for Heart Connection.)

Name _____   Date _____

Circle the appropriate box for each category.

Effort	Rhyme, Pattern, or Sound Words	Imagery	Line Breaks	Heart Connection
3	Strong sounding (ex., *Kerplunk!*)	Strong images	Strong breaks (ex., *A forget-me-not as if I could*)	Strong feel
2	Fuzzy sounding (ex., *It dropped.*)	Fuzzy images	Fuzzy breaks (ex., *And . . . and . . . and . . .*)	Fuzzy feel
1	Sounds like a story	No images	Looks like a story	No feel

We keep our drafts stapled together as we continue working on our poems and moving through new lessons. During conferences, I regularly refer to the students' drafts to show them how they are changing, revising, and adapting their poems. For example, Graciela's first draft about her baby brother was in narrative form: "He always breaks my stuff and he cries all the time and he pulls at my hair and it makes me mad. He's supposed to be cute and nice but I love him anyway." After we talked about repetition and line breaks, she rearranged her words like this: "He always breaks my stuff. He always cries. He always pulls my hair. He makes me mad but I love him anyway."

When Graciela and her partner looked at the rubric, Graciela saw that she had some imagery and repetition, but the heart connection was not strong. We read poems by other writers and realized that if she talked directly to her brother in the poem it might evoke stronger emotions. Graciela's final poem was this:

> *Baby Brother*
> *Don't break my stuff.*
> *Don't pull my hair.*
> *It's okay.*
> *I love you anyway.*

Giving and getting feedback in the primary grades may be the first time some students realize they have control over their accomplishments. Most students enjoy seeing how they have made changes and decisions to improve their work, but not all students will want to revise their work. I have come to see that choice is part of the lesson as well. For students who decide to leave their work as is, I reinforce that they are making a choice and that they will have no one to hold responsible except themselves for the outcome. Learning to accept responsibility for our actions is an important skill for all students, whether in writing, mathematics, or friendship. (See Figure 12.3 for an example of students collaborating by using rubrics.)

Figure 12.3
Adolfo uses the poetry rubric to give Jessica feedback.

Chapter 13

TRANSFORMATION

Every year I order monarch butterfly eggs before school starts. I love to have the caterpillars crawling around on the first day of school because it immediately engages the children in the true purpose of school: wondering, questioning, growing, and changing. And every year, I am mesmerized by the metamorphosis that takes place in that tiny chrysalis. Several times a week, after all the children have gone for the day, I find myself staring silently at the black and orange creature folded within that clear paper-thin shell. I am wonderstruck that we nurtured and fed and cared for a tiny crawly thing that transformed into a glorious flying creature of beauty. It truly is a miracle.

I'm sure you know where this analogy is going. Corny, I know, but so true nonetheless. Every year when students walk into my classroom, I stand just as much in awe at their potential as I do with the butterflies. I don't see punctuation lessons or fraction drills or famous American biographies. I see Robinson's story of going to see the Easter Bunny at the mall and forty exclamation points that follow because he understands the purpose of punctuation. I see a birthday cake drawn on paper, with lines dividing it equally, because Emma Ly wants to make sure her friends all have a "fair share." I see Bella's newspaper article about her grandparents overcoming difficulty because great leaders like Martin Luther King Jr. had to persevere too.

Our motto at Bailey's Elementary is "Create, Inquire, Connect," and it drives all our instructional decisions. How do we make the curriculum relevant, engaging, and connected so our students are using the knowledge to further their learning? We spend the week before school questioning, discussing, and creating connections for students. We use our weekly professional learning community meetings to look closely at student work to be sure we are supporting them in these connections, and we spend hours upon hours talking with one another about how to reach each student's individual potential. During the school year, as we are pressured to teach this standard today, reach that benchmark tomorrow, and give that assessment (every day, it seems!) in the future, we keep our students in the forefront of our lessons and strategies.

CREATIVE APPLICATION

At the end of the year we establish a museum where classes create individual projects that exemplify our school motto. One year, Christy Hermann Thompson and I had our students interview their parents about their cultures. They wrote questions in Writing Workshop, recorded the answers at home, and created a slide show on the computer. Some of the students had parents come in to share how to apply henna or make a tortilla. There were dozens of ways to present their learning at our Family Celebration. As a class, we painted fence posts that depicted the typical dress of a culture or the flag of a native country, adding these treasures to the butterfly garden that surrounded the playground (Figure 13.1).

Another year we designed a creative movement piece with coteacher Lorena Cervantes about the Underground Railroad. Creative Movement is one of the specialized programs at Bailey's that helps students connect their learning through the arts. Once a week students attend class in the Black Box Theatre to deepen their understanding of a subject and create a physical moving representation of their learning. Students have

Figure 13.1
The butterfly garden at Bailey's Elementary School

created pieces about the pumpkin's life cycle, about the rain forest habitat, and about famous Americans.

The year we created the Underground Railroad piece, the students worked to understand the hardship and fear of slavery as well as the joy and empowerment that came with freedom. We expanded the students' vocabulary with words such as *yearning, desperation, safe haven*, and *exaltation*. We read books such as *Henry's Freedom Box* (2007) by Ellen Levine and *Moses: When Harriet Tubman Led Her People to Freedom* (2006) by Carole Boston Weatherford and tried to fully understand the characters' lives and feelings.

Lorena helped the students put these words and emotions into movements that reflected their daily lives. She started with common injustices that happen on the playground—being left out or being teased—and the students moved their bodies to show that pain. Lorena then moved to celebratory events such as birthdays and Christmas morning. Again, the children internalized these emotions and displayed positions and movements that reflected their feelings. They had to control their bodies, be responsible for fully understanding the purpose of their movements, and show kindness when someone stumbled.

Soon we delved into *Martin's Big Words* by Doreen Rappaport (2007), about Martin Luther King Jr., reading and rereading to fully grasp the power of Dr. King's speeches. Each session built on the social and emotional skills of self-control, kindness, responsibility, and perseverance while strengthening students' connections to literacy standards such as comprehension, writer's voice, and character development. As students discussed and revised their group project, they demonstrated how their ability to hold a line of thinking, respectfully disagree, and incorporate new ideas into their personal schema had increased. Lorena says, "It was a magical time. They gave of each other, their movements were truthful, and they fed off each other's emotional honesty. The respect the children had for the work was deep."

The final piece of work was magical: Twenty-one six- and seven-year-olds crouched down in a field, hiding, seeking, and trembling. Students cast as slaves, slave owners, runaways, or supporters portrayed desperate fear and empowered peacefulness. (I get goose bumps remembering it.)

MAKING A DIFFERENCE IN CHILDREN'S LIVES

Throughout this book, I have stressed the importance of explicitly teaching children the social and emotional skills that will enable them to be successful in school and throughout their lives. Yet I know that some teachers and administrators still might say they do not have time in the overloaded school day to add one thing more. They may deceive themselves into believing that if they make classrooms more rigorous or reinforce more rules they will succeed in keeping the academic train on track.

You and I know differently. When students do not know how to regulate their social and emotional behavior, they will invariably use ineffective, unproductive, and disruptive ways to get their needs met. We must teach them how to name and fulfill their desires while considering the needs of others in order to have respectful and productive learning environments. These are not separate tasks. Rather, by teaching the emotional language with the social skills, we can layer on the academic content and have successful and rigorous discussions, questions, discoveries, and achievements that go far beyond any scripted curriculum.

When a student enters our classrooms and has no letter recognition or basic math facts, teachers ask, "How can I help?" Yet when a student shouts out or teases others verbally, we tend to place blame: "If her parents disciplined her more . . ." "If his parents weren't divorced . . ." Or my guilty one, "If she were my kid, this would not be happening." What we really need to do is ask, "How can I help?"

In Vivian Paley's book *The Kindness of Children* the author speaks with teacher Jerry Flambeau about the ordinary kindness of children. "We become witnesses," Jerry says. "We see who we are teaching, we see who we are playing with, we see who we all might be" (Paley 1999, 28).

While writing this book, I moved to upstate New York and became a substitute teacher for a year. I worked in five different schools, and in every one I saw social and emotional skills being taught. One classroom had a sign outside the door that said "Friendships Matter Here." Another had a poster with the words *THINK before you speak* written across the top and an acrostic of the word *THINK* going down the page:

T is it True?
H is it Helpful?
I is it Inspiring?
N is it Necessary?
K is it Kind?

In one school a special classroom program was designed to help students with severe social and emotional struggles. These children were unsuccessful in the general education classroom, but a special education teacher and a school psychologist believed they deserved to be part of the school community. The teachers worked closely with two other assistants to provide consistent and successful interactions for the students. They used the book *Have You Filled a Bucket Today?* (2006) by Carol McCloud as a cornerstone for their classroom expectations. McCloud's message encourages children to express appreciation, kindness, and love every day.

As a substitute teacher in this classroom, I witnessed the power of learning social and emotional skills. Gavin (not his real name) was an angry child who had great difficulty controlling his outbursts, but through this program he had gained self-control and was functioning quite well. One day, while the class gathered on the carpet for a math lesson, Gavin was on his assigned square but three of his classmates were not. Gavin's arms began to shake. He stood up and clenched his fists and squeezed his eyes shut until the teacher asked in a soothing tone, "Gavin, I see you're upset. What is happening?"

With his eyes still shut, Gavin said, "I am feeling squished. People are too close. I need to go to my desk." He proceeded back to his desk for a minute. The teacher helped the other students move to their appropriate spots and then she asked Gavin if he'd like to come back. "Yes, please," he replied. He returned to the carpet and the math lesson began.

This incident might seem small, but it was monumental. There would have been NO math lesson for anyone if Gavin had not learned the skills of identifying how his body was feeling and what he could respectfully do to help himself. These specialized teachers had worked intensely with Gavin so he realized he had the ability to make choices and decisions that made him feel peaceful.

The teachers shared with me that they do not have all the requirements set by New York State or the school district. They have "permission" to use social and emotional skills as the curriculum—and it works. Think of how many more Gavins we could help if we adapted and embedded the same explicit skills and vocabulary within the state and district curriculum requirements that we face in the general education classroom.

HELPING BUTTERFLIES SOAR

Christy and I went back to Bailey's Elementary because some of the students we taught for three years in a multiage classroom were graduating from fifth grade and moving on to a new school. We knew we probably wouldn't see them as a group in the future and we wanted to connect collectively one more time. We met our former students on the playground. In between many hugs and smiles, the children bantered about our time together:

- "Do you remember growing the bay grasses?"

- "Remember when we had the butterflies?"

- "I remember wearing our sandwich boards to promote our Poetry Slam."

Christy and I couldn't keep up with all their memories, but how we treasured hearing them! Toward the end, as the crowd of students thinned out, I caught a glimpse of Ezequiel. As a five-year-old he was inquisitive and eager to learn but did best with one-on-one discussions. He was not a joiner. That afternoon Ezequiel was standing just outside the group enjoying the memories and stories from his peers when I heard him comment, "Yep, good times. Those were some good times."

REFERENCES

Agee, Jon. 2005. *Terrific.* New York: Michael di Capau Books.

August, Diane, ed. 2006. "Developing Literacy in Second-Language Learners: Report of the National Literacy Panel on Language-Minority Children and Youth." Mahwah, NJ: Lawrence Erlbaum. http://www.cal.org/projects/archive/nlpreports/Executive_Summary.pdf.

Bang, Molly. 2004. *When Sophie Gets Angry—Really, Really Angry . . .* New York: Blue Sky.

Boelts, Maribeth. 2009. *Those Shoes.* Somerville, MA: Candlewick Press.

Brach, Tara. 2014. "Awakening from the Trance of Unworthiness." *Inquiring Mind* 17 (2). http://www.tarabrach.com/articles/inquiring-trance.html.

Bronson, Martha B. 2000. "Recognizing and Supporting the Development of Self-Regulation in Young Children." National Association for the Education of Young Children. http://www.smccd.edu/accounts/franciscoe/ece260/Promoting-Self-Regulation.pdf.

Burke, Anne. 2010. *Ready to Learn: Using Play to Build Literacy Skills in Young Learners.* Ontario, CA: Pembroke.

Calkins, Lucy. 2003. *Poetry: Powerful Thoughts in Tiny Packages.* Portsmouth, NH: Heinemann.

Chase, Penelle, and Jane Doan. 1996. *Choosing to Learn: Ownership and Responsibility in a Primary Multiage Classroom.* Portsmouth, NH: Heinemann.

Civic Enterprises, John Bridgeland, Mary Bruce, and Arya Hariharan. 2012. *The Missing Piece: A National Teacher Survey on How Social and Emotional Learning Can Empower Children and Transform Schools.* Report commissioned by the Collaborative for Academic, Social, and Emotional Learning (CASEL). Chicago: CASEL. http://www.civicenterprises.net/MediaLibrary/Docs/CASEL-2013ForumMediaRelease.pdf.

Clay, Marie. 1988. *By Different Paths to Common Outcomes.* Portsmouth, NH: Heinemann.

———. 1991. *Becoming Literate: The Construction of Inner Control.* Portsmouth, NH: Heinemann.

Coles, Robert. 1997. *The Moral Intelligence of Children.* New York: Random House.

Committee for Children. 2014. *Second Step: Skills for Social and Academic Success.* www.cfchildren.org/second-step.aspx.

Concordia University. 2014. "Five Stages of Second Language Acquisition." *Journal of News and Resources for Teachers*. http://education.cu-portland.edu/blog/news/five-stages-of-second-language-acquisition/.

Denton, Paula. 2005. *Learning Through Academic Choice.* Turners Falls, MA: Northeast Foundation for Children.

———. 2007. *The Power of Our Words: Teacher Language That Helps Children Learn.* Turners Falls, MA: Northeast Foundation for Children.

Denton, Paula, and Roxann Kriete. 2000. *The First Six Weeks of School.* Greenfield, MA: Northeast Foundation for Children.

Dewey, John. 1897. "My Pedagogic Creed." *School Journal* 54. http://dewey.pragmatism.org/creed.htm.

Eastman, P. D. 1961. *Go, Dog. Go!* New York: Random House.

Edwards, Nancy. 2001. *Glenna's Seeds*. Washington, DC: Child Welfare League of America.

Falk, Beverley, ed. 2012. *Defending Childhood: Keeping the Promise of Early Education.* New York: Teachers College Press.

Fatum, Barbara. 2013. *Healthy Classrooms, Emotional Intelligence, and Brain Research.* 6 Seconds. http://www.6seconds.org/2013/05/29/healthy-classrooms-emotional-intelligence-and-brain-research/.

Fillion, Sarah, et al. 2005. *Apology of Action and Literacy: Skills That Grow Together*. Responsive Classroom Newsletter, November. https://www.responsiveclassroom.org/article/apology-action-and-literacy.

The Franklin Institute. 2004. *Stress on the Brain*. Resources for Science Learning: The Human Brain. The Franklin Institute. http://www.fi.edu/learn/brain/stress.html.

Gallas, Karen. 1994. *The Languages of Learning: How Children Talk, Write, Dance, Draw, and Sing Their Understanding of the World.* New York: Teachers College Press.

Gould, Elaine, and Butler Knight. 2009. "Behavior Strategy: Focusing on Academic Enablers." William and Mary School of Education. http://education.wm.edu/centers/ttac/resources/articles/challengebehav/behaviorstrategies/index.php.

Green, Christopher. 2000. *A Theory of Human Motivation, A. H. Maslow (1943)*. An Internet resource developed by Christopher D. Green, York University, Toronto, ON. ISSN 1492-3713, Classics in the History of Psychology. Originally published in *Psychological Review* 50: 370–396. http://psychclassics.yorku.ca/Maslow/motivation.htm.

Gurian, Anita, and Ruth Formanek. 1983. *The Socially Competent Child.* Boston: Houghton Mifflin.

Hart, Betty, and Todd Risley. 1995. *Meaningful Differences in the Everyday Experiences of Young American Children.* Baltimore, MD: Brookes.

———. 2003. "The Early Catastrophe: The 30 Million Word Gap by Age 3." *American Educator.* American Federation of Teachers. https://www.aft.org/pdfs/americaneducator/spring2003/ TheEarlyCatastrophe.pdf.

Hart, Sura, and Victoria Kindle Hodson. 2004. *The Compassionate Classroom: Relationship Based Teaching and Learning.* Encinitas, CA: Puddle Dancer.

Heard, Georgia. 1989. *For the Good of the Earth and Sun: Teaching Poetry.* Portsmouth, NH: Heinemann.

Heard, Georgia, and Lester Laminack. 2008. *Lessons for Climb Inside a Poem.* Portsmouth, NH: firsthand Heinemann.

Horn, Martha, and Mary Ellen Giacobbe. 2007. *Talking, Drawing, Writing: Lessons for Our Youngest Writers.* Portland, ME: Stenhouse.

Hoyle, Rick, ed. 2010. Introduction to *The Handbook of Personality and Self-Regulation.* Oxford, UK: Wiley-Blackwell. http://onlinelibrary.wiley.com/doi/10.1002/9781444318111.fmatter/pdf.

Jensen, Eric. 2005. *Teaching with the Brain in Mind.* Alexandria, VA: Association for Supervision and Curriculum Development.

———. 2009. *Teaching with Poverty in Mind.* Alexandria, VA: Association for Supervision and Curriculum Development.

Johnston, Peter. 2004. *Choice Words: How Our Language Affects Children's Learning.* Portland, ME: Stenhouse.

Kadhiravan, Subramanian, and Vijayaraghavan Suresh. 2008. "Self-Regulated Behaviour at Work." Special Issue, *Journal of the Indian Academy of Applied Psychology* 34: 126–131. http://medind. nic.in/jak/t08/s1/jakt08s1p126.pdf.

Katz, Karen. 1999. *The Color of Us.* New York: Henry Holt.

Krashen, Steven. 1988. *Second Language Acquisition and Second Language Learning.* Upper Saddle River, NJ: Prentice Hall.

LeBon, Tim. 2011. "Abraham Maslow—Father of Humanistic Psychology, Self-Actualisation, the Hierarchy of Needs and Peak Experiences." http://www.timlebon.com/maslow.htm.

Levine, Ellen. 2007. *Henry's Freedom Box: A True Story from the Underground Railroad.* New York: Scholastic.

Lui, Angela. 2012. *Teaching in the Zone. An Introduction to Working Within the Zone of Proximal Development (ZPD) to Drive Effective Early Childhood Instruction.* Northwest Evaluation Association. Children's Progress. http://www.childrensprogress.com/wp-content/uploads/2012/05/ free-white-paper-vygotsky-zone-of-proximal-development-zpd-early-childhood.pdf.

Madonna. 2003. *Mr. Peabody's Apples.* New York: Callaway.

Mandela, Nelson. 1995. *Long Walk to Freedom.* New York: Little, Brown.

Marion, Marian. 2008. "Helping Young Children Manage the Strong Emotion of Anger." *Early Childhood News*. http://www.earlychildhoodnews.com/earlychildhood/ article_view.aspx?ArticleID=449.

Marr, Deborah, Mary-Margaret Windsor, and Sharon Cermak. 2001. "Handwriting Readiness: Locatives and Visuomotor Skills in the Kindergarten Year." *Early Childhood Research and Practice* 3 (1). http://ecrp.uiuc.edu/v3n1/marr.html.

McCloud, Carol. 2006. *Have You Filled a Bucket Today? A Guide to Daily Happiness for Kids.* Northville, MI: Ferne.

Mermelstein, Leah. 2007. *Don't Forget to Share: The Crucial Last Step in the Writing Workshop.* Portsmouth, NH: Heinemann.

Mind Matters. 2010. "Self-Regulation." Mind Matters. http://www.mindmatters.edu.au/ resources_and_downloads/staff_matters/the_thriving_self/useful_information/self-regulation. html.

Moses Guccione, Lindsey. 2012. "Oral Language Development and ELLs: 5 Challenges and Solutions." Washington, DC: Colorín Colorado WETA. http://www.colorincolorado.org/ article/50910/.

National Association for the Education of Young Children. 2009. *Developmentally Appropriate Practice in Early Childhood Programs Serving Children from Birth Through Age 8.* https://www. naeyc.org/files/naeyc/file/positions/PSDAP.pdf.

Neuman, Susan B., and David K. Dickinson, eds. 2011. *Handbook of Early Literacy Research, Volume 3.* New York: Guilford.

Nichols, Maria. 2006. *Comprehension Through Conversation: The Power of Purposeful Talk in the Reading Workshop.* Portsmouth, NH: Heinemann.

———. 2008. *Talking About Text: Guiding Students to Increase Comprehension Through Purposeful Talk.* Huntington Beach, CA: Shell Education.

Nidich, Sanford, et al. 2011. "Academic Achievement and Transcendental Meditation: A Study with At-Risk Urban Middle School Students." *Education* 131 (3): 556–564.

Northeast Foundation for Children. 2007. *Responsive Classroom Level I Resource Book.* Turners Falls, MA: Northeast Foundation for Children.

Nuckols, Cardwell. 2010. *The Ego-Less SELF: Achieving Peace and Tranquility Beyond All Understanding.* Deerfield Beach, FL: Health Communications.

O'Neill, Alexis. 2002. *The Recess Queen.* New York: Scholastic.

Otoshi, Kathyrn. 2008. *One.* San Rafael, CA: KO Kids Books.

Paley, Vivian Gussin. 1981. *Wally's Stories: Conversations in Kindergarten.* Cambridge, MA: Harvard University Press.

———. 1992. *You Can't Say You Can't Play.* Cambridge, MA: Harvard University Press.

———. 1999. *The Kindness of Children.* Cambridge, MA: Harvard University Press.

———. 2010. *The Boy on the Beach.* Chicago: The University of Chicago Press.

Parker, Emelie, and Tess Pardini. 2006. *The Words Came Down! English Language Learners Read, Write, and Talk Across the Curriculum, K–2.* Portland, ME: Stenhouse.

Parr, Todd. 2009. *It's Okay to Be Different.* New York: Little, Brown.

Partnership for 21st Century Skills. 2008. *21st Century Skills, Education, and Competitiveness: A Resource and Policy Guide.* http://www.p21.org/storage/documents/21st_century_skills_education_and_competitiveness_guide.pdf.

Payton, John, et al. 2008. *The Positive Impact of Social and Emotional Learning for Kindergarten to Eighth-Grade Students. Findings from Three Scientific Reviews.* Collaborative for Academic, Social, and Emotional Learning (CASEL). http://www.lpfch.org/sel/casel-narrative.pdf.

Peck, Jan. 1998. *The Giant Carrot.* New York: Dial.

Peterson, Ralph. 1992. *Life in a Crowded Place: Making a Learning Community.* Portsmouth, NH: Heinemann.

Phillips, Louise. N.d. "The Role of Storytelling in Early Literacy Development." B.Ed. paper. http://www.australianstorytelling.org.au/txt/childhd.php.

Pierson, Rita F. 2013. *Rita F. Pierson: Every Kid Needs a Champion.* Video file. https://www.ted.com/talks/rita_pierson_every_kid_needs_a_champion?quote=2143.

Pinkney, Andrea Davis. 2008. *Sit-In: How Four Friends Stood Up by Sitting Down.* New York: Little, Brown.

Polacco, Patricia. 1998. *Thank You, Mr. Falker.* New York: Philomel Books.

Pressley, Michael, and Christine B. McCormick. 2007. *Child and Adolescent Development for Educators.* New York: Guilford.

Randell, Beverly. 1995. *Wake Up, Dad.* New York: Houghton Mifflin Harcourt.

Rappaport, Doreen. 2007. *Martin's Big Words: The Life of Dr. Martin Luther King, Jr.* New York: Hyperion.

Raver, C. Cybele, and Jane Knitzer. 2002. *Ready to Enter: What Research Tells Policymakers About Strategies to Promote Social and Emotional School Readiness Among Three- and Four-Year-Old Children.* New York: National Center for Children in Poverty. http://www.nccp.org/publications/pdf/text_485.pdf.

Responsive Classroom. 2012. "Want Positive Behavior? Use Positive Language." https://www.responsiveclassroom.org/article/want-positive-behavior-use-positive-language.

Roseberry-McKibbin, Celeste. 2012. "The Impact of Poverty and Homelessness on Children's Oral and Literate Language: Practical Implications for Service Delivery." From a presentation at ASHA (American Speech-Language-Hearing Association) Schools Conference. Milwaukee, WI: California State University, Sacramento San Juan Unified School District. http://www.asha.org/uploadedFiles/Poverty-Homelessness-Childrens-Oral-Literate-Language.pdf.

Rosenberg, Marshall. 2003. *Nonviolent Communication: A Language for Life*. Encinitas, CA: Puddle Dancer.

Scanlon, Liz Garton. 2009. *All the World*. New York: Beach Lane Books.

Schertle, Alice. 1995. *Down the Road*. New York: Houghton Mifflin Harcourt.

Schweinhart, Lawrence, et al. 2005. *Lifetime Effects: The High/Scope Perry Preschool Study Through Age 40*. Ypsilanti, MI: High/Scope.

Seligman, Martin E. 2006. *Learned Optimism: How to Change Your Mind and Your Life*. New York: Vintage Books.

Sendak, Maurice. 1963. *Where the Wild Things Are*. New York: Harper & Row.

Shoda, Yuichi, Walter Mischel, and Philip K. Peake. 1990. "Predicting Adolescent Cognitive and Self-Regulatory Competencies from Preschool Delay of Gratification: Identifying Diagnostic Conditions." *Developmental Psychology* 26 (6). American Psychological Association. http://bingschool.stanford.edu/pub/wmischel/115-Dev%20Psych%201990.pdf.

Spires, Ashley. 2014. *The Most Magnificent Thing*. Tonawanda, NY: Kids Can Press.

Steig, William. 1986. *Brave Irene*. New York: Square Fish.

Suskind, Dana. *Project ASPIRE: Addressing Language Disparities for Children with Hearing Loss*. http://listeningandspokenlanguage.org/uploadedFiles/Connect/Meetings/2013_LSL_Symposium/Handouts/Project%20ASPIRE%20Addressing%20Language%20Disparities%20for%20Children%20with%20Hearing%20Loss.pdf.

Teaching Tolerance Project. 1997. *Starting Small: Teaching Tolerance in Preschool and Early Grades*. Montgomery, AL: Teaching Tolerance Project.

Thich Nhat Hahn. 1998. *The Heart of the Buddha's Teachings: Transforming Suffering into Peace, Joy, and Liberation*. New York: Broadway Books.

Thrangu Rinpoche, Venerable Khenchen. 2001. *The Twelve Links of Interdependent Origination*. Transcribed by Gaby Hollmann, trans. Ken Holmes, ed. Kate McDonnell. Crestone, CO: Namo Buddha. http://www.rinpoche.com/teachings/12links.pdf.

Tough, Paul. 2013. *How Children Succeed: Grit, Curiosity, and the Hidden Power of Character*. New York: Houghton Mifflin Harcourt.

Tschannen-Moran, Megan. 2004. *Trust Matters: Leadership for Successful Schools*. San Francisco: Jossey-Bass.

University of California–Los Angeles. 2009. "Conversing Helps Language Development More Than Reading Alone." *Science Daily*, July 17. www.sciencedaily.com/releases/2009/06/090629132204.htm.

Vygotsky, Lev. 1978. *Mind in Society: The Development of Higher Psychological Processes,* ed. Michael Cole, Vera John-Steiner, Sylvia Scribner, and Ellen Souberman. Cambridge, MA: Harvard University Press. http://www.ulfblanke.de/downloads/activity_theory/vygotsky1978.pdf.

Waddell, Martin. 1995. *Owl Babies*. Somerville, MA: Candlewick.

Wang, Fang, et al. 2013. "The Effects of Tai Chi on Depression, Anxiety, and Psychological Well-Being: A Systematic Review and Meta-Analysis." *International Journal of Behavioral Medicine* (September). http://link.springer.com/article/10.1007%2Fs12529-013-9351-9.

Weatherford, Carole Boston. 2006. *Moses: When Harriet Tubman Led Her People to Freedom*. New York: Hyperion.

Winter, Jeanette. 2008. *Wangari's Trees of Peace: A True Story from Africa*. New York: Houghton Mifflin Harcourt.

Witkin, Georgia. 1999. *Kid Stress: What It Is, How It Feels, How to Help*. New York: Penguin.

Woodson, Jacqueline. 2001. *The Other Side*. New York: Putnam.

Worth, Karen, et al. 2009. *The Essentials of Science and Literacy: A Guide for Teachers*. Portsmouth, NH: Heinemann.

INDEX